KRAV
SUCCESS

Turning Your Passion Into A Successful Business

by Jon Bullock

Jonathan D. Bullock

The right of Jonathan D. Bullock to be identified as the author of this work has been asserted in accordance with 77 and 78 of the Copyright Design and Patents Act 1988.

ISBN 978-1-5272-2823-8

Designed, and produced by Jon Bullock & James "Badger" Thompson

Edited by Alia Coster, founder of Coster Content Ltd.
www.costercontent.co.uk, email: info@costercontent.co.uk.

Printed in Great Britain

Krav Maga Success: Turning Your Passion Into A Successful Business

Dedication

To my Mum, for her forever love and
supporting my taking a different path.

To my Grandmother, the most selfless women I ever
met, you are deeply missed, yet you would not like the
way the world is turning out, rest in peace Nan.

And to HC, we had a lucky escape.

Acknowledgements

This book would not have happened if I had not met, and spent time with some amazing people.

To Eyal Yanilov, Zeev Cohen, Ray Hutchin, Allie Alberigo, and Rory Miller for their continued guidance.

To the team at Krav Maga Elite, who are always leading from the front.

And of course James Thompson, (aka the Badger) who's always watching my 6.

My eternal thanks to you all.

Foreword

It's been over 30 years since I started the mission of spreading the teachings of Imi Lichtenfeld and the system of krav maga to the world.

During these years, I have travelled close to 200 days a year, and made a living from teaching and built a global organisation.

It has been far from easy, and yet the present day sees more krav maga professionals making a living from their schools, with Krav Maga Global represented in over sixty countries.

In an ever-changing and uncertain world, the need for krav maga training continues to expand, and the demand for high quality and successful schools is bigger than ever.

To achieve success, instructors must balance their education in teaching the system with that of learning how to operate a successful business. Creating a stable and enduring base which can support students with a positive environment to grow and develop and learn the critical life skills of krav maga training.

Although the principles of krav maga are unique, the principles of running a business are not.

Excellence in anything you wish to master is about consistency, pushing through the low points and learning from the right people.

Jon has helped many of our school owners around the world and continues to be at the forefront of both krav maga training and business development within the organisation.

I hope you will focus, and study the valuable information shared in this book, by learning from someone who has taken his passion for krav maga and turned it into a successful business.

KOL TUV

Eyal Yanilov

June 2018

Contents

Introduction

I genuinely believe that you must find a way to live each day by spending your time doing the activities that set your heart on fire. When you discover a way to turn your passion into your income, you begin living an enjoyable, fulfilling life. You start to put yourself in control, and best utilise the precious time you have on this spinning planet.

If you're already on this path, my hat is sincerely off to you. You are part of the rare few that made it. But sadly, I've met so many people around the world - especially among my fellow krav maga instructors - who aren't. That doesn't mean they wouldn't love the opportunity to do so. The truth is, most people have everything they need right in front of their eyes. Sadly they excuse themselves from not doing what is necessary by blaming their lack of success on irrational fears — Or they are just unwilling and lazy.

There are no two ways about it. Over time, as technology has become increasingly prevalent, we've become soft. Physically, we've had less to adapt to and so we're losing our resilience. No longer do we have to go out and chop wood on a daily basis to build the life that we want. We've developed an impatient microwave mentality attitude where we want everything now. We're more inclined to find excuses not to do something. And then we are masters at blaming others for our lack of success or inabilities. As they say, patience is a virtue. And like any skill, it's an undervalued quality that we must practise.

Many people I've met are in the pursuit of success. Yet when I ask them to define what that means to them in simple terms and they can't. Most people associate success with anyone that appears to be living a bigger or better life. They usually measure these 'enviable' levels of achievement by someone who seemingly has more money and status than them. But here's the thing. Money is just a number. And numbers never end. There will always be the opportunity for more. There's one exception to the rule, one resource that you only have a finite amount of. Time.

To me, success is being clear about what you want. It's also about enjoying the process of getting there. It's never a straight road; there's always going to be hurdles to overcome, regardless of how far along your business journey you are. One way to measure your progress is to evaluate how your daily tasks leave you feeling. On most days - yes, even the hard ones - do you love what you're doing and how you're investing your time? Are you creating the life you want? If so, you're on the right path. Learn to be satisfied with what you have. Do not chase more if you cannot define what more is, or why you want it. Thinking in this way will drive you insane. As you grow older, this may turn in to regret; a feeling that must be avoided at all costs.

One key lesson I learnt early on is that the majority of the world care only about themselves. Most people aren't interested in the in's and out's of your personal and business life as much as you think they are. Except for your close circle of family and friends, no one is looking at you or thinking about your progress. There's no group of people judging your every move, sneering at you when you make a questionable decision. So relieve yourself of the burden of worrying what those around you think. Because hey! They probably don't. And that's a good thing.

I wrote this book as a guide to share how I successfully grew adult krav maga schools. By sharing my experiences and the challenges that have shaped my learning, I hope they assist you on your journey too.

I hope this book will challenge you, and if nothing else, it confirms to you - that regardless of how good you are at krav maga - there are so many factors you cannot hide from when running your own school. There are elements that you must learn and excel at. You'll need to push your personal boundaries of self-development. Some aspects you'll immediately love doing. Others you'll have to suck it up and do out of discipline; a common cost of going into business for yourself.

If you're already on your journey and things are going ok, why not carry on reading anyway? There is a difference between being ok, and being fantastic. Hopefully, you'll uncover a few golden nuggets from "Krav Maga Success: Turning Your Krav Maga Passion Into A Successful Business" that you can apply to your own school. If you're currently stuck trying to overcome frustrating hurdles, by making the small changes outlined in this book, we can defeat them together. I hope I can help make your business journey clearer, straightforward, and of course, more enjoyable.

"There is no group of people judging your every move. Focus on doing what you love!"

Chapter one

It's all about the adventures.

"Life is about exploring what's possible."

It was a dreary Sunday morning in late September 1997. I'm standing on the train platform in the small British town of Bury St Edmunds.

As a small rural town, Bury isn't really famous for much. It was a pleasant place to grow up though. After meeting in Lincolnshire, my parents moved down to Suffolk to be closer to my Father's family. It wasn't long after that I was born that my mother's parents followed suit. Then my brother came along, and the whole family uprooted and settled in Bury St Edmunds which became the place we'd grow up.

My mother was a talented nurse, progressing to become a sister in the Accident & Emergency department. She eventually had to take a step back in her career to have my brother and I. My father was in the car industry, selling car parts to consumers and businesses. He was a traditional man; working much of his life for the same local company.

If I'm honest, I don't remember much about my childhood. The memories that I can recall have served me well over my career. Lessons I'll share with you over the following pages as they've been pertinent to my achievements; and hopefully, will contribute towards yours.

Over the last few years, I've read countless books on personal development. One of the biggest lessons that I've learnt is that your past does not need to shape your future. That's not to say I had a terrible childhood, but it wasn't without its ups and downs. The most significant moment for me was when my father left my mother for another woman.

In some ways, this was a sad and emotionally challenging time for us, and deep down, I believe his actions affected me more than I care to admit. A double edge sword really, because at the same time, had this moment in our lives not happened, this book would never have been written. It's the critical life experiences that have ripple effects on our future. Had my past not played out the way it had, say, my father stuck around, my life would have followed a very different path. In some respects, I'm eternally angry at my father for breaking my mother's heart. At the same time, I'm grateful for the opportunities that the circumstances unlocked for me.

My father died of cancer in late 2017. The one thing I've pondered is if I should have told him how I felt. That although the consequences of his actions were painful, I wouldn't have changed a thing. I also wonder if he already knew that. Having seen him a few times over his final year, I came to realise that he'd created a new life. My mother, brother, and I had become his past. Only during his illness did we become significant again. Regardless of how things played out, he was still my father and had it not been for him, I'd not be here. Rest in peace Dad.

Back to my story. I'm on the platform edge with my baggage at my feet. I remember staring at the information board, acknowledging that I only had three minutes left. This is it. Standing next to me is my Mum, and all things considered, she's managing to keep strong.

I remember the conversation as if it was yesterday. "Remember, if you need anything we can always send it to you." Yes Mum, I know, I'm sure I've got everything. "And remember to…" Yes, I'll call you as soon as I arrive.

Through the mist of the morning rain, I see the headlights of the train approaching, the creaking of the locomotive crashes through the deafening silence of the station. There weren't many other commuters making their way down to Hampshire at 8am that particular Sunday morning.

The train slowly stops at the platform, I press the button to open the door and put my bags inside. I turn to my mum, and it's all become a little too much. The tears are starting to roll down her face as she bid me farewell with a tight squeeze and a "keep safe".

As we pull away from the station, the reality starts to kick-in about the adventure that lies ahead. As I waved to my mum, I held back the tears. I wanted her to know I was ready for this, and it was the right decision. When she was out of sight, I cried my eyes out like a four-year-old child.

Back then I didn't really give much thought to how my Mum felt. I was 18-years-old and excited about my new career. In contrast, she was in her 40's, watching her first-born son - who she had raised alone - leave to join the British Army.

Most people join the Army just to, well, join the Army. I wasn't like that. I believe in having clear plans. To me, it's vital that you know precisely what you're doing. More importantly, you need to know why you're doing it. I'd thoroughly researched my options, undertaking rigorous due diligence to ensure I made the right decision for me.

I knew I wanted to be a protector of some sort. That was the easy part. The challenge lied in discovering in what capacity I wanted to do it. I always had this urge to look after the people around me and make sure things would always be alright. Maybe this arose from growing up in a single-parent household. As the eldest son - whether you admit it or not - when your father leaves, you automatically become the man of the house. It's your responsibility to look out for everyone.

Regardless of where the desire to protect came from, it was a deep-rooted urge that drove me, and I always knew it's what I needed to do as a career.

First, I applied to be a police officer. I was quite rightly told that (at the time) there was no need for 18-year-old officers. Instead, they needed people with life experience. I had very little of that. I then researched joining the Navy and becoming a Royal Marine. While this presented itself as an exciting career, I saw little immediate transferable skills that I could use in the civilian world. I thought to myself "if I ever wanted to leave, what would I do, and how would this experience help me?"

At times, I've questioned my approach to life. Whether forward-thinking is a useful skill, or if I should try living more in the here and now. Ultimately, I feel my method has served me well. I've seen so many people make quick decisions that (without knowing) have shaped their future into something that they thought it never would be. Planning is one thing, and absolutely yes, you can over plan. But there is a difference between micromanaging every decision and thinking smartly. Which, in my opinion, is an invaluable skill.

A lot of people that join either the Military or the Police do so without clear reasons as to why they are entering. It's certainly not a job you do for recognition. Or the pay for that matter. Instead, your purpose comes from a higher, ideological place. It always starts out like this, yet much like any large organisation, people become disillusioned as to why they joined, then things change. Their why becomes the security that comes with the job; a far cry from the reason they joined in the first place. A common phrase that I often heard in the Military was "only ten more years until I leave." Imagine a group of people waiting a whole decade until retirement so they can have a pension payout. I've never understood the mindset. No amount of money can create happiness or the perfect lifestyle. To me, there's no such thing as job security any more. Anything could have happened in that time. So wasting my time working hard for a safety blanket that doesn't exist sounds crazy.

I realise that's a negative statement, and of course, it's not the case for everyone. That doesn't dispute the fact that it is a standard way of thinking. The armed forces and the police service are made up of some incredible people. The point that I am trying to arrive at is that if something in your life no longer seems right, enjoyable, or the reasons why you do it are no longer evident, then maybe a need for a change is in order. Changing your situation has to be a better solution than hanging around, waiting for a lump of money. You can always earn more money. It's time that you'll never get back

Next on the 'possible career' list was being a civilian bodyguard or close protection operative. There were very few courses around at that time, but I found one that really stuck out. After discussing the course with the business owner, it seemed fantastic, but then the situation was similar to trying to join the police. The owner said he'd happily take my money and train me, but as an 18-year-old bodyguard, it's unlikely I'd find any work. It was hard to hear at the time, but I'll always appreciate and respect his honesty.

Although I believe you can do whatever you want to do, choosing the right way to reach your goals is critical to give you the best chance of success. You may start down a path, and it changes, or have to take a longer route to get there. To me, this is smart thinking and adapting to your circumstances.

Between the marines, the police, or becoming a bodyguard, no option screamed out to me as the right one. My gut feeling told me there was something else that would be more ideal.

Which is when by chance I discovered a regiment in the army called the Royal Military Police. A police role within the Military? And, they had a specialist unit for close protection operations. It was undeniable. This was the job for me!

The Royal Military Police (RMP) or the 'Redcaps' is a police service to soldiers and their families. They carry out the same purpose as the civilian police, dealing with the same types of crime on a daily basis. They also have specialist roles from special investigations, to drugs intelligence, as well as close protection details supporting both Military operations and diplomatic missions at various embassies around the world.

The RMP close protection course is one of the most respected courses of its kind. It is eight-weeks in duration and has a high rate of failure due to the exceptionally high standards that were required to pass the course. If you wanted to become a close protection operative, you had to push and work hard for it. You had to be a clear thinker and a fast decision maker. Not to mention good with a firearm.

I served just under seven years in the Royal Military Police. The majority of which I spent on close protection operations protecting both Military officials and UK diplomats on overseas missions. I had some fantastic experiences, travelling around the world, meeting and working alongside some truly incredible people. Some of which I'm proud to say are still friends to this day. Anyone who has served in the Military will know, you might not see your ex-colleagues for years, but when you do, it's like you last saw them yesterday.

One colleague, Lee, a hugely experienced operator and somebody I admired and looked up to for guidance during my close protection career once said to me, "Jon, life is simply about adventures." A phrase that has stuck with me to this very day.

I believe life is about choices, about venturing down a path that will fulfil you; ensuring that you live every day happy. Many people say "I just want to be happier." I've never understood that phrase. How can you be happy, but want to be happier? In my opinion, you're either happy, or you're not.

I believe many people spend their daily life, thinking like they are going to live forever. They don't respect how precious time is. It's not like money. Money comes and goes. Sometimes you have more. Sometimes you have less. In contrast, when you lose time, It's gone forever. Every second, of every hour, of every week that passes, you'll never get back. How you use that time is so critically important. Entrepreneur Garry Vaynerchuk states: "...one reason you should do what you want in life, map out your journey and stick to it is simple. You are going to die!" Make every moment count.

CHAPTER CHECKPOINTS

Are you clear on your end goal?

Do you plan carefully?

What do you value most?

Chapter two

Asking the right questions.

*"Confidence to do big things is built by
asking those around you for help."*

My Military career came to an end while serving with 177 (Support) Platoon; a small team dedicated to the close protection of senior Military officials in Northern Ireland. It was there that I had that moment. The moment when a chain of thoughts triggered me to question whether a full career in the Army was for me. I had my doubts and started to feel like it was time for a new adventure.

I've always believed in observing the status quo and doing the complete opposite. Don't ask me why; I never realised I was consciously doing it until a few years ago. Following this way of thinking has almost always got me the results that I had wanted in many situations.

Let's face it. Three meals a day, a roof over your head, and a job for life gives us the security that we crave, and is daunting to think about losing that. For most people, the Military is a security blanket. This way of thinking snares a lot of Military personnel into a trap. Most people I knew were just looking to finish their service and retire. It would have been easy to fall into that way of thinking, but I chose not to.

It's common for people to make quick decisions based on emotional responses. To me, it represents almost a cry for help, in some situations, it can be seen as attention seeking. I see it as a form of communication, a message to others that you're happy to change things suddenly without a thought or care about the consequences. Erratic behaviour like this makes people around you feel uncomfortable while leaving you feeling temporarily in control. This rush of power only lasts for a fleeting moment. The people recover, and the feelings that led you to that rash decision burn out, and you are left justifying your irrational choices. Even worse, you have that sinking "oh no. What have I done" sensation.

It's wise to pause and reflect. Get some paper and a pen and write down the pros and cons of the dilemma you're facing. Let your adrenaline run its course. Then start to ask the right questions to the right people to make an informed and intelligent decision. Smart decisions are rarely made when you're angry, happy, or upset. Or when falling in love for that matter. Remember to breathe, slow down, and then honestly think about where you're at and what you want.

There is one thing I believe very few people understand about obtaining advice. It's not enough to merely ask a question. You must ask the right questions.

A great example of this is a conversation (unbeknown to me at the time) that would dramatically shape the path to the new adventure I'd eventually take after leaving the Army. I wanted to find out the opportunities that were out there in the private close protection sector. I'd heard about exotic assignments and big salaries and wanted a piece of the action myself. The question I posed to my colleague was: "What is the single, biggest factor stopping former RMP operatives finding their ideal private close protection job?" "Knowing different languages." He said. "The big companies with the big contracts prefer people who can speak a second language, ideally French or Spanish."

Had I just asked a simple question about the market and what it's like getting a well-paid job out in the private sector these days, he'd have probably just given me a simple answer and told me how the industry is tough to tap into.

Two years down the line, I'd become fluent in French so that when it came to leaving the RMP, I'd be a desirable candidate for a quality private close protection job. Without having taken the time to ask the right question, I'd have been in the same pool of talent as everyone else. You can do the same. Find the significant information that gives you the winning edge and helps you make the right decision for your business or personal goals.

A lack of the right information is, in my opinion, the reason most businesses fail. Without it, you cannot entirely make an informed decision. Especially when growing a business, as this can often lead to decisions that would not have been taken had the question been asked in a way with a clearly defined outcome.

The other thing I realised when he told me about being able to speak multiple languages was that I knew that most people wouldn't have gone out and actually done the legwork. They would consider it too hard or too much effort. They would give the excuses of no time or money to justify not doing it.

Remember what I said about doing the opposite to others? While deployed to North Africa, I paid for a local French tutor. I attended various language schools in France when I was on leave, and found a local tutor in Northern Ireland while I served my final year. I wanted to get the best job I could, and I was willing to play the long game to build my skills, knowledge, and experience to get there.

My next adventure had been set; I just didn't know it yet.

I followed my decision to join the Army because that's the path I had chosen, for clear reasons. However, it didn't mean that my destination couldn't change. Life should be an adventure. When you start to wonder what if, it's time to think about making a change.

There is no one making up the rules, but dream stealers will tell you otherwise. You know the types. The people who say, "you can't do that" or, "it won't work", or "people just don't do that", "but what about the pension, the job security?" The list goes on.

People are very good at imparting their negative opinion upon others through their fear of being left behind. If you can balance the fear of change with the feeling of excitement, then you'll find your world becomes a lot bigger. You need to be willing to focus, commit, work hard, and sometimes sacrifice to achieve what you want.

I had some fantastic learning experiences in the British Army. However, when I knew my time was up, I decided the pension and retirement were insignificant to my future. It was time for the next chapter to start.

CHAPTER CHECKPOINTS

How do you best cope with change?

Do you ask smart questions?

Whose opinion do you value?

Chapter three

From Russia, with love.

"Watch the behaviour of successful people, you'll learn a lot."

"You get what you wish for", is a common phrase used to explain success or achievement. Others will define this by dream, believe, achieve. If you focus on something, it becomes your reality. Whether the phenomenon is scientific, spiritual, or chance, it's something I very much believe in.

That's precisely what happened to me. Once I had made the decision to leave the Army and seek a job in the private close protection industry, things started to fall into place.

One morning, I was standing in the Platoon office in Northern Ireland when the phone rang. A colleague of my mine answered the phone. "177 (Support) Platoon, Rob speaking how can I help you?" Rob then shouted across to me. "Jon, you speak French, don't you? Come and take this phone call." Rob handed me the telephone and explained it was a former member of the platoon, with a job opportunity in the civilian sector. So I took what turned out to be a life-changing call.

That phone triggered a chain-reaction of events. I had a series of personal interviews with some very influential people in the corporate world, including two French-language assessments to see if I was suitable for a close protection job where I'd be living in the UK, yet frequently travelling to France.

Wow. Did that just happen?

Leaving the Army was just a difficult as joining. The unknown was awful. So was the feeling of discomfort thinking about leaving a world where everything is set out for you. However, it proved to be one of the best decisions I'd ever made.

For the next seven years, I'd work directly for a Russian billionaire as part of a small close protection team responsible for various security and intelligence tasks. All of my colleagues were former Royal Military Police close protection operatives, so the camaraderie remained the same, and everyone had an exceptionally high level of training.

To grow as a person and achieve what you ultimately desire you need to put yourself in situations that scare you. Ones that make you uncomfortable. Leaving the Army did just that. Most people spend their time in easy circumstances and shy from the idea of embracing change. Their inner critic makes them think that any break in routine will always be a bad thing. They take comfort in the familiar, and they would rather be unhappy than risk what might happen if they were to change it.

This is fear presenting itself in many ways. One of the common phrases to explain fear is: False Expectations Appearing Real.

It's a lot like sparring or grappling in krav maga. If you want to improve, train with the person who scares you the most, not the person you know you can easily beat. Staying within your safe zone will never help you grow.

In the UK there is a famous award-winning martial artist and writer called Geoff Thompson who always says: "in life, in training, and in business, there is no ability to grow and get better if you feel comfortable." Reading Geoff's books pushed me to actively seek discomfort. I don't like the feeling, but I understand it. Every time it has driven me to be better.

Our Russian client was an impressive man. Subtle, unassuming yet with a brain the size of a planet. In his late thirties, he was listed as one of Forbes Top 10 wealthiest people in the world. He was a man of few words, yet his strong presence in a room commanded respect. We worked directly with him. It really was an ideal job; rare in the private close protection industry.

It's easy to judge those who've created enormous wealth quickly, especially in such circumstances as the collapse of the Soviet Union and the privatisation of Russian industry under the Presidency of Boris Yeltsin. I won't go into Russian political history. Let's just say it was a turbulent time. Enemies were made, people died, and few came out on top.

I made it my decision not to judge his path to success. I'm not naive enough to think that all money earned in this era was made ethically. However, I'm sure you had to be brilliantly minded to survive. Especially when your only chance was to fight for what you wanted.

So rather than judge, I choose to observe this smart guy and see what characteristics shaped someone who had grown a large, multinational company, and who now had a net-worth of 28 billion dollars. I never had access to sensitive information on a day-to-day basis. Only when it was need-to-know. Usually when directly related to a set task or if it was security, or travel related. I didn't have a personal relationship with him either; he wasn't the kind of guy you'd sit around and chew the fat with.

For me, I was fascinated with observing his behaviour. 58% of human communication is in your body language. You can tell a lot by how someone deals with life by looking at his or her use of eye contact, and other non-verbal cues. A subject I've grown passionate about and have studied in-depth. My findings now form part of a conflict de-escalation programme that I have delivered to some of the largest companies in the world. Google, YouTube, and Facebook are just a few of them.

We provided a very discreet level of close protection to our client, balancing the need for him to live a normal life while making sure that he, his family, and his colleagues were safe from physical and information-based threats.

He took everything in his stride, he never appeared hurried or rushed. That doesn't mean he didn't get frustrated; it just meant that his pace of action was methodical. Decisions were made with a clear mind and thoroughly analysing the information available to him. He always took his time.

There were three critical things that I observed about our Russian client that I took as something to model:

- He never rushed anywhere;
- He was acutely aware of his surroundings; and
- He valued money.

When you watch a man with billions of dollars in the bank checking the cost of a pair of jeans in a high street department store, it's all too easy to think "just buy all of them". This is small minded thinking. Knowing the value of everything and whether you're paying a fair price was, I'm sure, a strategy he used in every aspect of his life. Regardless of whether it was trading commodities, buying an aeroplane, or simply purchasing a pair of jeans.

There is a common misconception that money breed's happiness. Having spent seven years in the presence of people whereby money is everywhere, I can tell you that's not the case. Trust me. Money does not make you happy.

Problems and challenges are all relative. They happen at every level, regardless of status or wealth and let's be honest, the higher status and wealth you have, it's a greater distance to fall, and the landing is always much, much harder.

What I observed during this time was that his entrepreneurial mindset appeared to be about growth and progress. Material things were a reward, yet never seemed to be the focus. He spent little time in the many houses he had, and would never be seen in the newspapers or on TV showing his wealth like so many others who've amassed similar levels. That type of behaviour is purely about status, yet unfortunately, many people picture this to be the definition of success. I think this attitude can be misleading to others as to what it means to do well in life.

In times of crisis, you often see people's real character come through. Our client suffered significant financial losses during the credit crunch, and his immediate action was to reduce his personal life spending first, before making any business cuts. Houses were closed, projects put on hold, and private staff reduced. He took action to deal with the losses, took personal responsibility, and handled the issue. I was lucky enough to survive the cut. To see the process of decision and action taking place to meet the problem head-on was a huge experience. There was no burying his head in the sand. The media suggested he would not survive it; they were wrong. Resilience, dedication, and personal responsibility kept him going. There were some significant lessons to be learnt from my observations.

Our working pattern was complicated. We could have large amounts of time off and then suddenly be working for three or four weeks without a break.

With vast amounts of time off, there is a need to keep the mind active. After all, there are only so many times you can go to the gym in one day! Time is valuable, and I felt I was not using it, I was merely waiting to get called to work; living on somebody else's time. Planning anything was difficult, but as a young guy without any family commitments, this was not too hard to handle in the beginning. However, as I felt myself becoming increasingly bored, it became apparent that it was time for another change.

I decided to quit the job with the Russian client. When I made the call to our team leader, Richard to let him know of my intention to leave, I was standing on the front of a 70m Superyacht, floating off the coast of Sardinia in the middle of August. The sun was beaming down on my face as I looked down at the crystal clear waters below. When people hear that they immediately imagine me being paid to be in paradise and that I must have been crazy to want to leave.

It wasn't my paradise. It wasn't my yacht.

I am grateful for the experience. Because of it, I have a small goal to return to Sardinia one day. I'll hire a boat to moor off of the coast and sit there with the sun beaming down. I doubt it will be a superyacht. I don't want that level of wealth. I know that for sure. However, I will be there on my time, not somebody else's.

I probably could have met that goal already by now, but it's not time yet. There are a few more things to do before I feel I've earned that.

At first, Richard was initially shocked as in the close protection world this was a one in a million job, and he was right. After I explained the situation, he understood. I had thought about leaving many times before. I found the thought only came to me in highly emotive states. I was tired, or I had been away for a few weeks, or the job had been quiet. I don't believe this to be the right state in which to make a life-changing decision.

Three things control your state of mind:
- The language/words you use;
- What you think about; and
- Your physiology/body language.

After a four-week period at work, my language was negative, I was focusing on what I didn't like, and my body language was pretty clear. Not a good time to make a decision.

When the time was right, I felt strong, confident, and excited about the future. I had mapped out a new path. Carefully thought it through, consulted people close to me, asked some smart questions and formulated my decision. I knew I was feeling too comfortable, so it was time to move on.

For most people leaving a very healthy salary doing a one in a million job with frequent travel abroad was not sensible. It was hard to explain this decision, and to this day I still get asked whether I thought it was right to leave. I get the same response to leaving the Army. I'm always asked, "Do I regret walking away?"

Ask me those questions when I'm tired, cash flow in my business is low, deadlines are close, staff are not having a good day, mistakes have been made, and I'll probably reply, "HELL YES" while swearing a lot and going on a rant that makes no sense. However, I challenge you to find me a business owner that doesn't want to quit once a month. It's a perfectly normal emotional response, and I always know the feeling will pass.

There's a difference between momentary lapses of lack in your self-belief and repeatedly having outbreaks of emotional responses in front of people who are close to you or work with you. Be sure to keep the latter to a minimum. Seeing you getting angry, annoyed, and frustrated when the going gets tough and you start reminiscing about the good times can make you look flaky. A personality trait that can make your staff or someone supporting your krav maga school feel nervous and threatened.

Geoff Thompson says that self-defence starts with "defence against the self". Monitor your behaviour in front of others at all costs. Control these thoughts, de-escalate yourself, go for a walk, turn the laptop off, train krav maga, or go to the gym. Do not let them manifest into something bigger. You don't want irreplaceable staff members looking for a new job for fear the next sudden outburst might be their last.

Leaving the Russian job was when my journey to krav maga success began, as I had chosen to build a business out of my passion for martial arts training. A love that started at a very young age.

CHAPTER CHECKPOINTS

How do you deal with uncertainty?

Are you aware of your comfort zones?

How do you react during challenging times?

Chapter four

Good at the wrong sports.

"Focus on your strengths and delegate your weaknesses to people better than you."

Okay. I'll admit it. I was 'that boy' at school. Yes, it's true. I was terrible at sports. Football, rugby, cricket, you name it, I was crap. You know in the movies you see the kid left at the end that no one wanted on their team? Yep. That was me.

From a young age, I never really warmed to the traditional sports, the ones that were preferred by the sports teachers as they looked to see if the next David Beckham might be in their class. Purely in the hope they might be remembered and get interviewed on the local news 20 years later. You get the gist.

There was one exception though. I was pretty good at basketball. I played for the school and then my local town. A career that, let's face it, was always going to be 'short' lived. It's not like I'm the tallest guy in the room.

While the other kids were at the football club, my brother and I chose to start martial arts as our after-school activity. Our uncle had a friend who was involved in the local judo club, so we enrolled there and began practising.

Judo is an excellent system for early child development. Immediately it starts to improve balance, stability, and it's symmetrical - meaning you're continually doing repetitions on both sides - helping to reduce the asymmetries of the body. It also teaches you to fall in a way that limits injury, something you do a lot as a child and will probably do in your old age at some point. Judo isn't really a self-defence system, but back then, as kids, we didn't face the issues that children of today do, it was very different. In those days, there might be the odd pulling and pushing in the playground, or a punch if you were unlucky. Problems with knives and group violence were rare. It wasn't anything close to what it is today.

My brother and I were successful in judo, winning our weight divisions at different competitions and the open categories as well. In the open tournaments, the final match would always be between either myself or my brother versus one of the Stagg family, Robert and Lisa Stagg.

One year during an upset in the semi-finals, we had both defeated the Staggs, and it was now Bullock versus Bullock for the gold medal!

I guess you're now waiting for a play-by-play account of what happened during this grudge match. All I'm willing to say is that I won. However, my brother has a very compelling story about me "standing on his foot" before I threw him for the win. He suggests that underhanded tactics were at play. Unfortunately, the alleged malfeasance occurred before the rise of the iPhone so, in the absence of the necessary video evidence to support his claim, it is therefore unfounded. Now, where's my medal?

As I got older, I grew out of judo and was looking for something different. I'd discovered other martial arts, and when my judo instructor saw me practising elbow and knee strikes on one of the newer members of the club, a stern look from him made me realise that maybe my time in judo was over.

This was about the time that Jean Claude Van Damme was in his prime. When films like Kickboxer and Bloodsport inspired my brother and I. Not one person that trained in martial arts in the late 80's/early 90's can tell me you didn't practice your jumping kicks in your living room after watching a Van Damme classic for the 27th time. If you're making this claim, I don't believe you!

Eventually, I hung up my judo gi and joined a local kickboxing club along with four close friends from school.

I'd say this was my first exposure to a martial arts club that operated as a business. The judo club was noticeably run for the love of the sport. In contrast, the kickboxing club was a full-time job for the instructor. The club had a great community spirit, the instructor was unquestionably the leading man, and everybody looked up to him. As far as I know, he is still teaching today which would mean he is in his 60's and going strong. He was a devout family man, with many children (about eight I think!) They all trained in the club at some point or another. He was an excellent teacher - especially with children - he knew how to build their self-confidence, which was inspiring to watch.

Based on what I now know about growing successful schools, when I think back to the way he ran his club in the days of no internet, he did very well indeed. Building the club relied on the methods of advertising from leaflets, posters, newspaper articles and ads, and of course word-of-mouth recommendations.

Our original Kickboxing group slowly reduced to three, and then down to two until I was the only one still training. I had found my sense of belonging. I was training four or five times a week. It didn't matter to me what the lesson was - even if we were repeating the same one - I always saw it as an improvement.

The feeling of belonging is fundamental. We need to know that we are a vital part of a group. As my good friend and mentor Rory Miller says, "we don't survive well on their own, even the best lone survival experts in the world have their equipment made by someone else."

We are all members of various groups. Family groups, work, social circles, religion, and sporting clubs to name a few. But taking part isn't enough. We need to understand our position in these groups. Where do we sit? What is our level of importance? What do others in the group think about us?

We're not always happy in the groups we exist in, yet the fear of change or leaving the group becomes scary, so we'd rather stay and complain about it than risk the possibilities of the unknown.

Krav maga schools are strong groups. They have clear structures and progression models which provide a favourable structure to be part of. The use of a coherent grading structure allows people to know their position in the group. It also provides a reliable model for students to follow and measure how they are progressing in line with their fellow students and their personal goals.

But, it's not all positive. If someone does not pass a grading, they can be left feeling humiliated which in turn sees that individual getting upset, becoming negative, and even worse, quitting the school.

Successful schools need structure, something that an excellent grading system provides. It can be very powerful, or very damaging to your success. How you manage that structure is significant. When somebody new wants to join your school, knowing how their progress is monitored is essential.

However you promote or run grading in your school, please think about that for a moment. How do you grade? Do you provide the opportunity for people to increase their status and position in the club?

Failing a grading is never about the actual event itself. It's the feeling of humiliation and not being good enough after working so hard.

How do you help when your students' feel they have failed? Do you clearly communicate how they can progress? How do you deal with the situation of a students setback?

Your ability to deal with these questions shows your true talent as a school owner and instructor. Being able to recognise the value of being part of a group and what it represents to people is about so much more than the techniques that you teach. The same goes for us as instructors. We suffer the same feeling regarding our own progression. But you must be conscientiously aware of it to do something about it, rather than reacting when it happens.

When people find a group to belong to, they often become very protective of their peers. Think about it. How protective are you over your family group? Your friendship group? Or the football team you support? You will protect them at all costs, even if logically it makes no sense. We encourage teams that lose and support friends that do crazy things.

Even if being in that group is no longer a positive experience people still stay. Think of someone who won't leave an abusive marriage. Or the worker who remains in a job they hate for 20 years. Your krav maga school is a strong social group, ensure it's one that people do not want to leave. Make it clear that you're there to help. Regardless of results in grading or the challenges that a student has. It's also vital you make sure you progress people at the right pace that suits them in a way that limits disappointment and keeps them focused.

When somebody has been training in your school for a while, it's likely they are there for the long-haul. There will be some that leave as they fall out of love with the training, or feel they are not progressing. A definite sign that somebody is considering leaving is when they are still paying, but not turning up to class. You will be tempted to let them pay and say nothing, but that means the relationship has broken down. It's no longer a personal relationship, it's become transactional and change is coming. Do not allow this to happen, keep the constant contact and help people through the tough times. A big part of growing your school is learning how to limit the number of people who leave. Knowing why they are leaving becomes of paramount importance. For many of your students, quitting isn't an overnight decision. I can probably guarantee it had nothing to do with what they were learning either. There's always more to the story.

One of the most significant challenges to deal with is when a student leaves your school to train at another school. Don't get me wrong, sometimes this will be for a genuine reason. Maybe the family are relocating, but for the most part, students generally leave your school to go to another as something has occurred which has affected their status. Maybe they didn't pass a grading, or they feel you're stunting their growth. Another reason is that they believe they can do it better, and want to be top dog. They want to be the instructor: they want to be you.

A lack of variety is another factor that might rock students (or indeed your instructors) loyalty. I can't stress how important it is that to grow a krav maga school you have to continually balance the need for education versus entertainment in your lesson planning. Otherwise, your school will either be quite small, full of people who are dedicated to your way, or people looking for something fun before they get bored and move on, having learnt very little. But at least they can tell everyone they "used to do krav maga."

Helping people progress involves being clear on how people learn, what their goals are, and what they are looking to achieve. Back in the old days of martial arts training, showing up to class and doing whatever the 'Sensei' said was enough. I'm not saying that doesn't still exist. I'm saying that it's not a great basis on which to build a successful school. It leaves too much room for the mind to wander, and for students to quit hoping to find the 'fix' they are looking for elsewhere. People want to enjoy things, and the Sensei lead dojo doesn't always breed enjoyment. Just because something is enjoyable, doesn't mean it's not progressive.

On the contrary, competent coaching and instructing styles are critical to retaining students. Many people can do, not everyone can teach. Just wearing the instructor badge isn't enough to keep people coming back. One of the models I show in our schools is to recognise the difference between teaching, or merely talking at your students. These activities are categorically different and have a massive impact on the dynamics of the group.

Showing how much you know is just glorified bragging and doesn't help anyone. Trying to create carbon copies of yourself is a terrible strategy to retain students. Instead, teach them what they need to know at their level so they can be as good as they can be as individuals. Point out their strengths and how they can adapt training to suit them. Showing them you care and tailoring your teaching to them will keep them coming back.

Being a competent instructor takes endless forms. It might be as simple as respecting people's need to know "why" they are doing something. It's a pandemic in our society and is both a positive and negative trait to question everything. We live in a very untrusting world, where authority and experience are less respected, as the internet allows people to pretend to be something they are not. As a result, the "but why" question is ever more prominent. But also, some people just like to understand the mechanics of an action to thoroughly learn it.

How many things in your own life do you believe you probably should question, but you don't because you're afraid of the answer? Perhaps at work, you think a task you've been given doesn't make sense, yet you do it anyway.

What about trust? How many people in your life can you say you honestly trust? For example, for someone to walk past a homeless person on the street asking for money to buy food, and not to give any for fear they might go and spend it on alcohol makes no sense. Considering that same passerby is quite happy to get on an aeroplane and fly at 40,000 feet for 10 hours and just assume the pilot is not drunk. Trust is screwed up, so we ask "why" more often than ever. Sometimes founded through not clearly understanding something. However, it is usually due down to a lack of trust.

Your ability to teach effectively and to answer the why question before it is asked is critical. This is easily achieved through being authentic, genuine, and helping others become a better version of themselves through your training.

Back in my kickboxing days, I experienced my very own change in status, and for the first time, found myself not trusting the very person I'd committed so much time to. As a result, I learnt what it meant to maintain a group, keep my word, and as the leader it taught me the importance of being trustworthy, shaping the way I treat people in my schools to this day.

I was very committed to my kickboxing school, but my time came to an end when I chose to join the Military. I returned back to the school as much as I could when I was on leave. I was yet to achieve my black belt, and I was very determined to do this so I trained as much as I could when I was back home and eventually took my test. It was a very intense experience. I passed, and for me, this was a considerable achievement.

But then something happened. My instructor - who I held a tremendous amount of respect for and was a significant influence in my preparation to join the Army - moved the goal posts. He said that before my black belt was given to me, I needed to commit to consistent training for a set amount of time. Only after that would my belt be awarded.

I was pretty upset after hearing this, and as a young guy I couldn't quite work out why he would do this to anyone. As a confident Military man, I didn't want to accept it. I thought it was totally wrong, I had shown continued loyalty and commitment to the club, and I felt distraught for the lack of recognition. I put everything into achieving the belt, and I felt rewarded with humiliation. Something inside me pushed to do something about it.

For the first time in my whole kickboxing career, I stepped out of the group and contacted the governing organisation.

Back in those days, a governing body was a posh description for somebody who had bought bulk insurance from a broker, and set up an organisation/federation/association and was now selling it to various clubs along with some fancy certificates. There were no continuity training or professional standard. Something I'd later relate back to as inspiration on how not to run a business.

I contacted the governing body, explained the situation. They awarded me the certificate after seeing news about the grading in a national martial arts magazine. They felt I had earned it, but without the signature of my instructor, I felt it did not recognise my hard work; and that my dedication and didn't mean anything.

You may be wondering why my instructor held back the certificate. I'd been loyal and passed the test, so what were his reasons?

Unfortunately, he had a few of his previous black belts leave him in the past to set up on their own - while not all did so out of spite - it was excruciating for him.

As a survival precaution, we tend to do all we can to limit discomfort; especially when it affects us emotionally. Sometimes this lends itself to treating people in a way that they do not deserve. His past was painful, so not giving the black belt was his way of coping with his own ego. Not the approach I advise you take for your students.

Of course, there are just some things you cannot do anything about. Letting go is also something you need to get good at. Otherwise, it limits your growth as you're too busy focusing on the small from the past. Moving forward is the only solution, and I had to do that.

My kickboxing adventure came to an end. All of it was a valid experience and marked a time in my life that would set out what I'd do for a living in the future. I had already learnt so much about running a successful school, I just didn't know it yet. I'd seen how to build a community, but I'd also seen some of the classic mistakes that school owners made back then. Sadly those same mistakes are still being made today.

While having my black belt conditionally withheld stung my ego, it was a significant learning curve and the ground for which I laid the foundations of my krav maga success.

CHAPTER CHECKPOINTS

Does your school provide a strong social group?

How do you help others deal with set backs?

Do you focus on teaching or just talking?

Chapter five

Getting your PhD.

"Success is gained through becoming clear on your why and being able to communicate that to others"

With my kickboxing journey well and truly behind me, I began the search for a system that I could really connect with. Something that combined my love of training and my professional goals.

During my time in the Army, having travelled to many different countries, I experienced an array of martial arts systems, and I made it my mission to find the best fit for me.

I practised everything from wing chun kung fu with a very strange chap called Frank in the UK, Thai Boxing in Belfast with the fittest man I've ever met called Keith, and some weird Asian martial art (which I cannot remember the name of) taught by a local hero while serving in Afghanistan.

If there was a chance to train, I'd take it.

I figured out that traditional systems were not for me. I struggled to focus on repeating the same movement over and over again based on beliefs and concepts of problems that existed many years ago, yet are not so relevant now. I needed something current and evolving.

As for sporting systems, I'd been competing in judo and some kickboxing competitions since I was young, so I decided to leave them in the past.

I needed a system that was very clear on answering the 'why' question, and for that system to have direct answers. I've met and trained with instructors from various martial arts systems over the years, and I'm always analysing if they understand why they are teaching movements and techniques in a particular way. Can they then explain it simply to their students?

The answer of "because that's why my teacher did" isn't good enough. Your students need more than that. It won't help their progress by just doing. Understanding the why behind their actions is essential to their success. The human brain needs clarity, not confusion if the training is to be of use one day.

I sat back and thought about my goals and analysed why I wanted to find a new system.

I was a protector; I was used to working in challenging environments where learning practical, relevant skills were critical to survival. These may well have to be used in times where my adrenaline was running high. Extreme situations where I may have to make life-saving snap decisions without warning.

Typically, these decisions would have been how to best protect other people. Drawing on my experience, I needed a system that educated instructors in a way they could explain why they were doing certain things. It was critical to me because I knew that's the fundamental ingredient for students progress. That's when I discovered reality-based training.

I stumbled upon the Israeli system of krav maga. It utilised modern methodologies designed for the purposes of self-protection. I knew straight away I had found what I'd been looking for. It met all of my goals, and it seemed logical in design. If I could understand it from the beginning, it meant that others would too.

I hit the ground running from this point, and my passion shone immediately. Believing in your chosen career is absolutely critical. You might be talented enough to get students through the door, but if your heart's not in it, it will be noticeable. And you'll have a 'for sale' sign on your school before you know it.

I've met an abundance of instructors who've taken a short course to teach krav maga. They started teaching and promptly stopped. They quit because they hadn't invested the time working out if it was truly what they wanted to do. They didn't consider long-term plans and instead produced a bunch of excuses as to why they don't do it anymore.

In my opinion, when you don't have to earn a penny to get up and do what you do day after day you've found your calling. It's something you can't take away. It might go up and down as your emotional state changes, but it's deep-rooted in you. There's nothing you or anyone else around you can do about it. When it becomes your means to make an income? Even better.

There's a level of responsibility I believe one has as an instructor. If you're going to take people's money and time for something they are discovering a passion for, you had better be sure you're heart is in it. That's what real leadership looks like. Leaders inspire action. As leadership coach Simon Sinek says, "People don't buy what you do, they buy why you do it."

This starts from a young age. A child will always ask "why?" That doesn't change as we mature into adults. The question just becomes less about curiosity and more about establishing a connection of trust.

When you take on the instructor role, it's not longer just about you. One of the most significant powers of influence over others is having authority. People look up to you as a credible expert, for the most part, will like you, and over time, wholeheartedly trust you. They will follow your path, invest in your 'why', and blindly take your guidance. It's a huge responsibility to take. One that's full of benefits, but also a factor a lot of cereal box instructors overlook.

Which instructor are you?

While we all have our own personality traits and characteristics, you can boil a typical instructor down into one of four categories:

- Those that start and quit;
- The magpies;
- Those that went into their qualification haphazardly; and
- Those who care.

Those who start and quit.

This one is self-explanatory. These instructors tend to seek out another system. They stop because they don't believe what they teach anymore. Typically this suggests to me a lack of foresight. I'd argue they probably didn't understand the cost of success in the first place.

The magpies.

The instructors always looking for the latest or next best thing. They start learning another martial art or self-defence system before they fully understand the first one they started. They then begin to introduce these methods to their students, because it's fresh in their mind and what they are currently 'into'. Typically it contradicts what they have already learnt and its horrendously confusing. You'll find students will leave, you'll appear as 'a little bit lost,' and frankly, it's selfish. You're stunting your students' growth because you don't know what you want.

Those that went into their qualification haphazardly

These instructors we've already covered, those instructors who rushed into their qualifications because it looked 'cool', they could quickly feel important and were focused only on themselves, and not the role of an instructor.

Those who care.

That, dear reader, is you. A leader, someone who wants to inspire others

How does poor leadership reflect on your students? For one thing. It wastes their time. Our most valuable commodity. If you were a student and you joined a school, began training and after a few years, the instructor decided the system they had dedicated so much time to was now no longer any good you'd be pretty annoyed. It may be that your authority is as such that people just follow you, and that's possible, but deep down, you've taken these people off a path they started on, didn't consider their goals and just did what you wanted to do based on how you felt at the time.

I've seen this happen so many times. As people move from one system to another in search of the latest thing, and even moving from one krav maga organisation to another. Please stop this. Make the right decision early, do your research before committing and remember change is difficult for people, and it's not just about you.

If you think you might have tendencies of the other three instructors, think carefully before making changes in what you teach and who you study with. The impact has a massive butterfly effect. If you're in it for the long-haul, make a decision and stick to it. Limit the changes you make. Strive to be an influencer who helps to make things better. Not one always searching for the greener grass. I'll let you into a little secret. It doesn't exist. It's what you make of your circumstances and how you share that with others that counts.

There is nothing wrong with cross-training, I do it myself. I study Gracie Jiu-Jitsu (GJJ) for fun. The difference is, I do not let the skills learnt cloud my judgement when I teach krav maga.

If you advertise that you teach krav maga, but you actually teach another system or a mix of stuff you've learnt and merely use the name for marketing purposes, I believe this is unfair and misleading to your students.

Do what you say you do, be transparent and honest and let people decide what they want to do. If you're the person to teach them, they'll stay. A good example is mixed martial arts (MMA). MMA is a style in its own right. If you teach judo and kung fu and advertise MMA, sure you might be showing a mix of martial arts, but it's out of context, and that's misleading.

Successful business owners love what they do and are driven by their burning passion. I love the krav maga system. I love teaching it. I love showing others how I believe it can help them, and I love helping to improve it wherever I can. I'm in it for the long game. Are you?

Leading with self-belief.

They say your vibe attracts your tribe. Focus your efforts on students who want to work with your school, not wasting time trying to convince people on the fence. Self-belief is all that's required. You need to be clear about your why, and people will follow. People see your passion. It's infectious. It all becomes down to you realising and clearly understanding why you're teaching krav maga, and how that's communicated to others. This is the first thing that's needed for a school to be successful. Students need to see your enthusiasm, your passion. This must never be in question. Both online and offline. The amount of instructors who use social media to air their dirty laundry is astounding, and then they wonder why their schools are not growing and why no one wants to train with them.

Your 'why' must be clear, and you must be able to communicate that to anyone you come across, meet, work with or want to help. One of the best ways to practice your why is to practice the elevator question. I'm not sure who came up with it, but it's fantastic.

The idea is that if you were in an elevator with someone you didn't know and you had one minute or so in that space, and they asked that classic wedding reception question. "What do you do for a living?" How would you answer?

I struggled with this for so long. I never really valued what I did for a living. Through my upbringing and influences through previous roles, I learnt to believe that running my own krav maga school was not a real job. It's something I have an incredible passion for, but convinced myself you shouldn't enjoy what you do for a living as it was a prevalent belief in my circles. I was almost afraid to share what I believe.

For a long time, I'd really play down the answer to this question when to the point that it was almost embarrassing to the people I was with. I never seemed proud of what I did. The reality is, deep down it was all I cared about.

When you say to someone "I teach krav maga or self-defence", they often have a preconceived idea of what that means. That it's not a real job to earn a living and was really about making a little bit of cash on the side.

Through reading and spending time with the right people, I managed to break this pattern of limiting self-worth, and I proudly changed my explanation as to what I did.

"I'm the owner of the of a company that teaches a unique type of self-defence training to various different people, organisations, and groups all over the world."

Do not confuse telling the truth and being proud of what you're doing with boasting. They are entirely different things. As long as you're not mentioning money (the definition of bragging), there's nothing to be ashamed of.

When I changed my belief and my level of self-worth, I can honestly say that many things started to change for me. From the way I thought about my life, to the way I behaved around others and the sorts of people that I began to associate with. A positive change occurred, more opportunities came my way. I hadn't actually done anything differently. I was still the same person yet the perception of others had changed for the better as I was able to share what I believed and what I could offer.

Self-worth is very hard for people these days. Having taught krav maga for many years, I'd always ask people: "Would you be willing to do whatever was necessary to protect yourself?" Some people struggle with this question as they fight their views of what is right and wrong ingrained from their youth, wondering if they need permission, and often answer the question with a question, generally with a list of criteria to confirm before responding.

Yet if you change the question to: "Would you be willing to do whatever was necessary to protect somebody you loved?" The answer is almost always "yes, I'd do anything", and you can even see their body language change when they answer. Although a commendable answer, it's also screwed up as it shows a lack of self-worth. They are willing to do anything to protect somebody else, but when they have to defend themselves, they are going to wonder if doing what's necessary is allowed.

Everyone has the right to defend themselves just as everyone has the right to achieve whatever they want. You do not need the permission of others to follow your chosen path (so long as it's ethical.) There has been no better time to achieve your goals.

Be your best you.

Information is everywhere, accessible and free. Do not take it for granted and do not waste it. Go and become a student again.

If you ever had to defend yourself, then you may, at some point be judged by others. Yet if what you did was necessary, and you could explain what you did and why you didn't do something else; you'll be ok. That judgement is coming from a logical process of assessing facts.

Judgement by others in what you do for a living and how you spend your time does not come from the same, logical point of view, it's based on opinion, not facts. Respectfully, if, after understanding their point of view, I don't agree with their opinion - if it's about my life and choices and they are not a part of them - I'm not going to listen to them. And you shouldn't either.

This is pure emotion, driven by some level of jealousy or own belief that they, the judgemental ones, are not doing what they genuinely love and therefore have to transfer those feelings towards you. They do this to bring you down to their level of thinking. If you were to achieve what you wanted and move forward, how would that look on them? They might be forgotten or left behind, or be seen as less within the groups you share, and they can't allow that to happen. Remember, it's humiliating!

Ignore the naysayers and do it anyway.

Are you passionate about what you're doing? And if so are you communicating that to others by being clear on why you teach krav maga and how you can help them? This really is a crucial part of growing a successful school. Your students, your staff, and other instructors from around the world will feed off your energy.

One of the best marketing tools is word of mouth where people speak about you to others. It costs nothing, they choose to do it and for nothing in return. They buy into you, what you do, and why you do it. Respect that trust, keep being the best you can be and your school will grow.

Be proud of who you are, the path you have chosen and practice that elevator question to the point it makes people speechless and proud to be associated with you. Before you know it, the doors will (quite literally!) open. Trust me, it has happened to me many times.

As one of my fellow instructors Alan D says, you need to get your PhD in krav maga: passion, hunger, and desire. He's right. This attitude is, by far, the best platform on which to build your success.

CHAPTER CHECKPOINTS

Can you clearly answer a why question?

Do you love what you do?

How do you answer the elevator question?

Chapter six

Rockstars.

"Build a team of exceptional people; you cannot do it alone""

I had decided krav maga was the system for me. It ticked all of my boxes, so I needed to start to learn it to be able to teach one day.

During this time, only a few instructors were teaching in the UK. Pretty much all of them had been educated by Eyal Yanilov, as he was the pioneer travelling the world spreading the system.

The krav maga of today is very different, like most other systems, it is now quite splintered. As the ever-growing number of quick-fix solutions continue to be on the rise, the krav maga name has become diluted. But back then, there was really only one central organisation providing instructor education across the world. So there was a level of consistency and clarity about what the system involved.

There are generally two ways the martial arts industry qualifies instructors. By their time served and their rank within the system. When somebody reaches a certain level, they can become known as an instructor or assistant instructor. This will give your students something to work towards. Or, the other method is that they qualify through a structured phase of learning over an intensive period. Otherwise known as an instructor course.

Both of these routes have their pros and cons. Krav maga chooses to use the instructor course method, and there are now many around the world, most of which do not offer what they say they do. Be careful where you invest your hard earned money if you're reading this and thinking of attending. Check backgrounds, ask smart questions, and be rightly suspicious.

For you to grow your krav maga school, you need to come to terms with one the fact that your school cannot expand while you are doing everything. Finding qualified instructors to help you is critical and finding the best route to qualify the right people is extremely important. They will represent you, your brand, and what you believe in so choose wisely.

You need to understand that you being on the teaching floor, day in and day out and also being in the office, day in and day out, will not help your business grow. Your success becomes solely reliant on the number of hours you can commit to. Don't get me wrong. Reducing my hours was one of the hardest things I've had to do. I love teaching and if I could spend all day just helping people get better, I would. And yes, I have the choice to do that but it would be at the cost of growth of the school. I want to do it as a choice, not as a necessity. The more I grow as a person in my own learning around the business, the more people I can help.

If you choose to remain on the teaching floor and running all of the day-to-day school tasks, then I can pretty much map out for you the financial ceiling that your school will hit. After which it will grow no further. There is nothing wrong with that if that's what you choose to do. However having met many school owners over the years, the most significant thing they wished to be able to do is to teach when they want, to whom they wish to. Rather than having to teach all the time just to keep the lights on in the gym. You need to get to the point where you can, most of the time, do what you want to every day, with the odd day of doing things out of discipline but most of the time, having the choice.

There is a common phrase which says "a business is a commercial, profitable enterprise that operates without you."

Although I understand this phrase, and when it comes to growing multiple companies it makes sense. But that's not for me. I don't want the school to operate without me. It's what I do and what I love. Most business owners want an exit strategy, a way to sell the business. My exit strategy is to hopefully sell the school to someone who is part of the school, is dedicated and wants to continue the legacy that I set out. Until then, I want to be involved on my terms. Which means I need help if I'm going to do this long term.

If we analyse the real challenge of starting to work with others and growing other areas of the school, and supporting your team; it's not actually about not being on the mats. Quite the opposite. You actually have to give up an element of control to achieve your goals. To reach them, you need to build a team that you trust. Giving them the ability to make decisions so you can move forward together. You will need to fire yourself from specific roles in the school and let those great people do it much better than you can.

I always compare it to my close protection role. How useful would I actually be protecting someone on my own? The concept of the individual bodyguard (IBG) is flawed, yet people get away with this if the threat is low or they are tasked with other non-protective duties.

If there were a severe threat, a serious risk to a VIP we'd have a team of highly skilled people with access to protective technology and various types of transport to move us quickly from one place to the next. Everybody would know the plan. They'd know what the ideal scenario was when everything is running smoothly, and they'd also know the procedure when if it all started to go a little sideways. Above all, we'd be communicating all the time to make sure the operation was running well, to notice any threats ahead and deal with them as efficiently as possible. But if I was doing that alone, eventually I'm going to drop the ball, or reach my limit and then, how effective am I'm at protecting someone?

Your school is no different. It requires the support of highly skilled people who communicate and look out for each other. It needs technology and systems to make life easier, and everyone on the team certainly needs to know where they're going. You also need to be clear on your milestones and end goal.

Before you start building your team, and labelling people as assistant instructors, or offering them a place on an instructor's course, you need to understand the difference between skills and values clearly. Trust me. Not knowing this will cause you some severe pressure at some point in the future, and you'll end up making on the spot decisions which are not always ideal.

Values.

"To keep it simple: skills can be taught, values cannot."

How many krav maga schools do you know whose instructors break-away to open their own club under a cloud of black smoke? It happens a lot, and I believe it all comes down to values.

If you are very clear on what your personal and business values are, then these provide a guideline to vet the people you will choose to work with. A good rule of thumb to live by is that values beat skill. I can teach someone (within reason) the skills they need yet I cannot teach values. They are built into people, derived over time through social programming, (how they were raised) and experiences at a young age.

Before even considering working with or employing others, make sure you spend the time getting clear on your own values. It will save you a lot of time and money. I've lost a lot of both by choosing the wrong people to work with.

As Roy Disney said, "It's not hard to make decisions when you know what your values are."

There's a classic phrase, "but my krav maga school is different." I've heard this so many times. Sorry but it's not!

When a business advertises a job, they have a role and need to find the right person to fill that role. Rather than we have a person, let's find them a purpose. This may happen during an internal recruitment process where departments are moved around, but even if this is the case, and they know who they want to take the role, they still have to advertise it.

I've made the mistake of trying to find a role for a person so many times it hurts, and every time it's caused me pain at some point, whether immediately or long term, the fact I did it the wrong way around always comes back to haunt me. By far the best recruitment decisions I have ever made are from advertising jobs and then finding out who fits the role. This might sound really simple, and common sense. But when your school is growing, you are under pressure, and you need help, you will also make decisions through rose tinted glasses, just to take the pressure off. But it's a short-term solution, and the storm is coming.

Change your mindset when recruiting. I used to think, "Matt Smith is a good guy, he'd make an excellent instructor. I need another instructor." This approach failed me many times. Instead, try:

"I need another instructor, what are the skills and values we are looking for in an instructor?"

You also need to consider:

- What will their responsibilities be?
- What do we need them to commit to?
- What does the role involve?

If Matt Smith hears about this opportunity and wants to apply, good for him. You may even let Matt know about the opportunity, but you must do so in a way that it's a job opening, not one built for him. I cannot emphasise this enough. You might mention to him, "Matt, the school is looking to expand and is recruiting new instructors, if you'd like to have a chat let me know."

I'm a big advocate of reputable instructor courses to qualify people to teach rather than time served for one simple reason. I can select staff on people's values and then teach skills, rather than having to select on skills and 'hope' those few skilful people have the right values.

Always start with the end in mind. Notice who are the 'shining lights' in the school because when you are looking for instructors one day, you'll know their skill level is good enough to consider them for the position; so long as they want it.

If you find their values are a little off-centre from yours, it doesn't mean you don't appreciate them, you just realise they may not be the ideal candidate regardless of how skilful they are; especially for the long term. They might be ok in the beginning as it's new, but eventually, when it becomes a little more routine, their values will show and it may cause issues. The moment you mention an increase in status to somebody, to become an instructor it can do peculiar things to people you thought were once humble. I've seen some shocking changes in people through this opportunity,

To expand your business, you need help. Both in teaching and administrative support. Take the time to map out the role, and then see what type of person resonates with that role. If it happens to be your star student, you've hit the jackpot!

To help get you started, here's an idea of my business values:

- Commit;
- Focus;
- Lead;
- Learn;
- Be real; and
- Be limitless.

I don't need to ask too many questions these days. By observing the way someone behaves and listening to the words they use tells me a lot about their values. Values are a great checklist to start off the search for the next rock star to join your team.

Build a team: Together Everybody Achieves More.

When a new school starts out, everybody helps out. It's a journey. It's fun. The family might help out, friends, other instructors, even neighbours. I've been pretty lucky with getting help from those around me. I was even more fortunate that most of them had some additional skills: from social media to print design and the building trade. It made getting things done easier. Thankfully, we didn't need to outsource too much.

But there will come a time when just you and your instructors and some good Samaritans cannot do everything. You'll need to go and recruit more staff to help with the day to day stuff. This frees up more of your time and the time of your instructors. They can then focus on teaching your students and offering the best level of training possible. Recruiting non-instructing staff is scary stuff. It's no longer just you and a couple of others who share your krav maga passion, you are out looking for real people who want a real job. People who come to work for stability, an income, and want it to fit around their other commitments. This is a very different mindset to you and your instructors who just love teaching and training. The fact you get paid for it is a bonus.

With recruitment comes contracts, salary negotiations, holiday, sickness, pensions to name but a few compliance based subjects that need to be covered. However scary, if you genuinely want to grow your school, it has to be done.

Even though recruiting staff for admin or sales type roles is very different from finding an instructor to help you, the principles remain the same. They must resonate with your values, and you must recruit amazing people.

As I write this book, I currently have three instructors working in my primary school, and four non-instructing staff helping with everything from operating our online shop, managing our licensed schools, and supporting with the running our governing body; Krav Maga Global in the UK.

As we grow as a company, everybody's role is evolving, becoming more transparent or sometimes even changing completely, as they demonstrate an interest in a particular area of the business, or wish to learn a specific skill.

Day-by-day I see each of them growing in confidence and starting to share my passion for what we do. They might not know how to teach krav maga, but they realise it's a useful skill for people and that our company is focused on helping people as well as profit, and that resonates very well with them. I realised once I had employed more people, that providing jobs, careers, and a work-life balance to others is very rewarding and has since become a reason as to why I strive to grow and expand. I love giving people an opportunity and helping others. Again, it's my protective nature. I don't want to see good people struggle or suffer.

When I first started thinking about recruiting staff for office-based duties, I took time to establish how I'd attract the right people, and what sort of environment would suit them. I spent hours on this but then realised I was only thinking of me and what I'd need. Most jobs will advertise the exact hours, salary and conditions, and then will interview people as they apply. Yet most companies who follow this procedure seemed to end up with clock watchers; employees who sit and wait for the five to eight hours to go by so they can get on with their lives. I have been to many companies whereby productivity is measured by how long you are sitting at your desk. I can't think of a more ridiculous way of getting people to do stuff, so I changed my tactic and work on the basis that work is something that you do, not somewhere that you go.

I advertised online and through word of mouth referrals making sure I was clear about what the company was about, the types of people we were looking and loosely what the role would involve but with the caveat that it could also include other responsibilities as the company grows. I did not mention anything about working hours or salary, I just stated whether it was part time or full time. I started to meet a few people, and the first questions I'd ask are:

"What working hours would suit you around your family/other commitments?"

"What hourly rate are you looking for so that you can live comfortably without worrying daily?"

Each and every time I asked these questions, the candidate looked at me shocked and almost always replied "aren't you meant to tell me those things?" I had no idea what their life was like, so how could I possibly know that.

At this point you may be thinking "but what if they ask for ridiculous hours and a high salary?" Trust me, it never happens. Good people with good values simply want to work a fair day for a reasonable salary, work hard and then go do what they do when they are not at work. Few people come with the intention to get all they can out of it, and if you do meet people like that, you'll know within seconds.

I really believe that if someone has a job that reduces the stress in their lives, they give more of themselves. It might be that it allows them to look after their kids or a sick family member. Perhaps the money helps them save for the house they want or reach their goals. No matter what their reasons, if their values align with yours, they will work hard during the time they are there; quite simply because they appreciate it.

Unfortunately, we do live in a world of wanting to do as little as possible, but still expecting more. For every reward, you have to invest something. Typically, your time, effort, or your skills. By having a clear understanding of being fair, giving more than you receive and helping people to become better in the company, to learn more skills and, most importantly have a voice is critical. Regular team meetings where people share their views, and their opinions are listened to is a vital part of working together. In a successful team, everybody knows what everybody else does and that they can rely on each other to do their bit, so the ship keeps sailing and making progress.

Will it be a calm sea most of the journey? Absolutely not. There will be waves, and there will be small mutinies at times. But your role as captain is to keep your ship steady and keep it moving forward.

Recruiting and managing staff is hard. Paying wages every month is a huge responsibility; especially when you know that those wages feed their children, and help with their mortgage on their house or pay their rent. It's a big deal. But as long as you recruit rockstars, the challenges will be limited.

Appreciate them as a team, and as individuals, together, you'll move up to the next level.

There will be times when you find yourself having to let people go, whether by their own accord or because they are no longer doing what is expected. Toxic staff spread their germs, and it can bring everything down quicker than you realise. The best advice I was ever given was to hire people slowly and fire them fast. By taking the time to find the right employee on their values, you can avoid this happening, and the rockstars will show up.

And why do I call them rockstars? They make things happen, they shine, and they always give their best performance. Every single day.

CHAPTER CHECKPOINTS

What are you top three values?

How do you select potential instructors?

Are you a team player?

Chapter seven

It's my train set.

"Being an expert in krav maga does not make you an expert in business. Listen to others!"

Working with others is about letting go of a little control. It's tough. Believe me, I suffer. But it's all about having the right attitude and learning to be a good leader.

There is one phrase that I have heard many krav maga school owners say that irritates me beyond belief. It's typically said when one of your instructors or office staff may have suggested something you might not like, and they have questioned a decision you've made: "It's my train set."

Translated, this rather obnoxious statement means: "The school is mine. Not yours, do what I say." It means they really don't care what other people think about the school. They ignore the fact that taking onboard others opinions can have a positive impact. It helps you learn and grow, and makes your team feel a part of a community. Instead, if you hold this belief, you just look like a know it all. Being an expert in krav maga does not make you an expert in business. Another newsflash… you don't know it all. No one does.

Leadership is a critical skill in growing a successful krav maga school. This attitude suggests lousy direction. If you have it, you're destined to fail.

Your team is exactly that; they are a team. They all have various roles and responsibilities. Some of your team members may not be paid instructors or members of staff. They might be dedicated students who feel strongly about contributing to your club. If that's the case, be grateful. People are willingly giving up precious time to help you.

Change your way of thinking. Instead of being a dictator try becoming a strong leader. One that understands that they have a position within the team as well. To give support and direction to everyone, to be the risk taker. To back everyone up when things go well, and to help motivate people through challenges when things don't go quite as planned.

If there is one single skill that I believe all krav maga instructors and school owners must train, it is their ability to listen. By listening I mean doing so actively. Taking people's viewpoint and opinion on board and helping them move forwards; both personally and professionally. Learning to help others grow, will make you a much better leader and person yourself.

Nobody likes a dictator. Stomping your feet and commanding authority is short-term thinking. It's another example of lousy leadership as it means that nobody on your team feels they can share ideas or concerns for fear of being humiliated in front of the team.

A leader who uses the 'it's my train set' philosophy is spending their time protecting their status and position, rather than growing their school. If that's you, STOP. It's not moving you or anyone else in your team forwards, and you're preventing everyone from growing.

Unfortunately, we live in a world where perceived status overrides doing the right thing. In your schools' case, that attitude is awful and no good and benefit of the team. If you find instructors are often leaving and breaking away to open their own schools, or students are continually leaving to train somewhere else, you might consider re-evaluating your outlook.

Let the master become the student.

First and foremost as an instructor and school owner I'd recommend taking time to read about leadership, understand that people want to feel empowered to think for themselves and to feel liberated to make suggestions and try new things; knowing they have your full support.

Another phrase that I hear a lot of school owners say is: "That will never work. That's a waste of time."

If somebody has an idea, investigate it. I've covered not drastically making internal changes, but with that, I mean not switching what you teach or making sudden changes without thought.

Streamlining business processes or making classes more enjoyable will only have positive benefits. When someone makes a suggestion to improve your business, unless you clearly understand the concept and test the idea, how can you possibly know if it will work? The short answer is that you can't.

Take some time to reflect. If a member of your team wants to try something new, how do you respond? Do you immediately shoot that idea down because it wasn't yours? If so, I'm sorry to tell you this but you never even listened to their opinion, you just heard that it wasn't yours and reacted emotionally. You cared more about your status than seeing if it was a valid idea or not. Of course, I don't want to be presumptuous here because I don't know your end goals. If you're looking to make your krav maga school a success (as the title suggests) perhaps it's time to include the thoughts and opinions of those around you too.

Focus on your team and what's important. Understand that people have a voice and lead by example. Be a transformational leader; help people to become a better version of themselves and understand which of their human needs are most important to them. How do you do this? Talk to them. By asking them questions, their opinion will be abundantly clear in their answers.

Personal development author and coach, Tony Robbins says that all of us have the following six fundamental needs:

- Certainty.
- Uncertainty.

- Growth.
- Love/connection.
- Significance.
- Contribution.

For most people, two of the six needs are more important to them than others. For example, in myself, I know that uncertainty and growth are a big deal for me. I need to know that I'm always improving and developing. I like the thought of the unknown. I'm prepared to take risks.

For others, uncertainty is a terrifying thought.

Students who come to your krav maga school will all like the certainty of how you run your school and the processes that you follow, yet they need that little bit of uncertainty. That comes from the skills they learn in your classes. If all students knew exactly what was being taught, do you think they'd turn up all the time? Of course not. They need that element of surprise.

The grading systems in krav maga satisfy the need for growth to feel like you're moving forward. Of course, gradings also helps to boost significance. Don't take my word for it. Check your students' social media roughly three hours after they pass their next grading. They'll be seeking recognition (and quite rightly too!)

A connection is provided by being part of your school. It allows people to become part of a like-minded community with shared values and interests. It gives them the identity that they crave. Those students who want to become instructors, those who put the mats out each session and offer to help at events are significant contributors, they see value in doing their bit to help things become better.

When you can recognise the strongest of the six basic needs of your team members and students, it empowers you to make them better. To help them progress. If you meet the requirements of people, you'll have their loyalty for life. If you don't, it creates frustration and the feeling of stagnation, and they start to look elsewhere to get their needs met.

The same goes for your family and personal relationships. Most relationships in life break down as one of the people in the relationship failed to understand the strongest needs in the other, until it's too late.

Lead by example, listen and understand people. Drive them to make decisions, to be proactive and reward them in line with their human needs. Be the person who is willing to test things out and analyse those results. One of the most powerful things you can do is to send regular surveys to your students, your staff, and instructors, to find out what they think and discuss any ideas they might have.

When somebody suggests an idea, stop, think, and give a rational and logical response that shows you appreciate their point of view. If it adds value, why not give it a try?

Do not spend your time suffering from the disease we call 'sensi-itus.' You can't run your school on your own. You need a team and you need students. They need to be devoted. People are viciously loyal when their needs are met, they are given a voice, and they feel part of something bigger than themselves.

Create a safe haven for your students and employees. Make them proud to be part of your school in a way they want to commit to constant and never-ending improvement. Be an innovator for change and development and ensure that everyone has a fantastic time along the way.

To do that you need to first reflect on the type of leader that you are. By first fully understanding yourself, you can begin to understand others. The kind of leader that you think you might be may, unfortunately, be wrong. I fell into this trap, and it wasn't until I spent some time as part of a business group that the realisation hit that I wasn't who I thought I was.

Sixth Division, provided coaching and support on certain types of customer relationship management software systems. What they've achieved has blown my mind. They are exceptionally good at it and are one of the coolest groups of people I have ever met. They create an environment where their clients (mostly entrepreneurs) make their ideas and dreams happen.

How great is that?

Sixth Division also run a mastermind group, led by their CEO and Founder, Brad Martineau. Brad is a brilliant man who he has a compelling story to success. During one of the mastermind sessions, Brad explained a model of leadership that made me quickly realise that some swift changes in my leadership style needed to happen.

Brad explained that great leaders offer two things: challenge and support.

Depending on the type of the leader you are, the level to which you give of each drastically differs.

Which one are you?

The abdicator

The abdicator is the weakest of the leaders. They offer little support to their team, but they also ask very little of them, there is no challenge, no motivation given for the team to want to find solutions and even if they do, the support to see those ideas through is not there. If you know you're an abdicator, it's likely that your school is not very strong. Your instructors and other people who are working with you, will feel very unmotivated, but they are still there as they haven't found a better place to go yet; but they will.

The dominator

The dominator is a dictator. They want everything done, as fast as possible. When the team ask for help, they get nothing back. They challenge people then offer no assistance or guidance about how to achieve their targets. Almost setting people up to fail. Leadership is about giving direction, and support. The dominator rules the team and has an "if you don't like it, leave" attitude. They typically use fear and manipulation to get what they want; playing on the vulnerabilities of the people around them. Do not be this person. It won't make you very popular.

The protector

The protector offers a low level of challenge to their team, not allowing them to spread their creativeness. Instead, the protector favours to almost do the work for them or, finds reasons to not train others in the skill sets that they have for fear of them getting it wrong. I'm sure you're aware that nobody will care as much about your school as you do. It's also almost certain nobody will complete each task to the same level of unachievable excellence either. However, as marketing genius, Dan Kennedy would say, "good is good enough."

A protector works hard, looking after everyone, making sure everything gets done. In truth, it doesn't. In fact, many things get forgotten, balls get dropped, and you end up creating more work as you pick up the pieces. Please don't confuse being a protector with caring. They are two very different things. Caring is often letting people think for themselves, and being there as a guiding hand to help when needed. You can still care without being the saviour. Your job is to help others become stronger, not protect them from failure. Failure is a part of learning and growing stronger.

My goal is to shift from being a protector to the final type of leadership style, which is the most effective.

The liberator

The liberator offers both high support but also a challenge. This is all about helping people to be the best version of themselves that they can be. They help people to ask the right questions, and to come up with the correct answers. If people get stuck, the liberator will train them in weak areas, helping them to develop.

It has taken time, but I feel I'm moving more and more into this way of behaving. Don't get me wrong. The protector is a substantial part of me, so I often have to step back and realise that I'm falling back into that habit. When our company stops growing and gets stuck it's usually because we've had a lot going on, and I've started protecting again. It's a habit, it's not conscious, but I'm now aware of it.

But this isn't about me. As a school owner which type of leader are you?

If you're already a strong liberator, then you're way ahead of me in the game. If not, take time to work out who you are, and if it's helping or hindering. Evaluate how you behave with your team. Do you mother them too much, or do you give them far too much space, with no guidance at all? By identifying your style of leadership, you can begin to improve.

Work with the right people and lead them in a way that gives them the freedom to make decisions, making sure you are clear on the direction you're headed and how they fit into your grand plan.

CHAPTER CHECKPOINTS

Do you consider the opinion of others?

What is your leadership style?

What are your top two human needs?

Chapter eight

Walking away from 500K.

"Make big, scary decisions!"

Have you ever been travelling in your car with the opposite sex, and got lost? I mean completely lost. No sat nav. You're relying on an actual map. Old school, I know. The other person may suggest sensible ideas to get back on the right road to continue your journey. They want to help solve the problem and find a way that you can both get what you want, to get to the destination you planned to.

But it never really works out that way.

If a man is driving, and a woman suggests maybe asking somebody local for directions. Well, for us men, you just don't do that. We'd rather struggle on, looking at the map, or trying to fix the sat nav and waste more time than to do the logical thing of just asking for help. Especially from another man.

If a woman is driving, and a man suggests that you're lost, the retort is usually: "well maybe you should drive." We all know where that conversation is going.

My point to this is two-fold. Two people on the same journey want the same thing. To get to the destination they planned to reach. How you get there, however, will always include discussion, challenges or disagreements, and heated moments of differing beliefs.

Regardless, the destination remains a mutual one.

It's the same with a business partnership. Many school owners that I have met along my journey own their schools with another instructor. They might be partners on paper, but the reality is quite the opposite.

There are the exceptions of course, but generally, my experience in the krav maga world is that most partnerships - at some point

- breakdown, which then causes a lot of problems. Ultimately, the students - those individuals that trust your brand - suffer. If you are in a partnership or thinking about starting one, it's incredibly important you have your terms legally written down.

In the interests of clarity, the definition of a business partnership here is a 50/50 split ownership between two people. Giving them equal legal rights within the school.

Don't get me wrong. Business partnerships do work. As long as both agree on:

- The destination of the business;
- The vision of what the company will look like;
- What the company does;
- How it serves people; and most importantly
- The business values.

In the beginning, a business partnership that's 50/50 generally also means that the workload is evenly split between two partners. I know that's not necessarily true in all cases, but to help make my point let's assume that everything in the business is divided - in both reward and responsibility - between two people.

Like any relationship, a business partnership always starts out as exciting, new, fresh and with lots of plans, everybody is going to do their part in the business and make sure it works. Both people are going to work equally as hard. It's a nice thought. And a great way to start.

However, I can pretty much guarantee it won't stay like this, and when the balance shifts, it will likely cause severe upset within the partnership.

Starting as you mean to go on: equally.

For a krav maga school to grow - much like any business - the owners of that business must also grow in knowledge and understanding in various subjects. A krav maga school cannot overtake the owner. Meaning, the school cannot grow faster than the school owner's knowledge. It's up to you to become better at the unknown if you want your school to excel. You should be competent in finance, leadership, communication, marketing, team building, and many other generic business skills. Or you need to know and have the resources to delegate effectively. Being good at krav maga is not enough to run a successful school.

There comes a time during growth that you need to seek out help, advice, and more knowledge. This may be in the form of reading certain books, attending workshops or seeking help from a mentor or business coach. Somebody reliable to guide forward in your business. It's no different to getting a personal trainer at the gym. With your hard efforts and their in-depth knowledge, you become focussed and work efficiently towards where you want to be.

It amazes me how much time and money is spent by krav maga instructors in learning the krav maga system and how to teach, but hardly anything is spent on how to grow a school. In fact, most information on growing businesses is free online these days. Think about how much time you've spent on krav maga training camps, courses, workshops, and further knowledge. As an instructor, the idea is to spread that knowledge, to as many people as possible and hopefully, also make a financial return. It's beneficial to adopt the same approach when it comes to the running of your business.

If you're working in a partnership, and one person starts to learn and develop the skills needed to run a business, and the other does not, serious issues arise. Cracks begin to appear. One person is pushing their creative spirit; the other is happier as it is and the tension that comes, as a result, creates a frustration gap that massively impacts the school.

My first adventure of owning a krav maga school was after completing my krav maga instructors course. I was full of energy, I had quite a lot of free time due to my work in the close protection private sector, as I often had pockets of time between travelling.

During the krav maga instructors course, I met a group of like-minded people. One guy already had an existing krav maga school, and the other four had the desire to set a school up after completing of the course. We all decided to work together and start a new school. There were only a few in the UK at this time, and they didn't seem to be doing very well. We firmly believed that we could do a better job.

At the time, we had a plan. Neil - the guy who had the existing school - would merge with our new school, creating a bigger one off the back of an already established brand.

The four of us set the company up as shareholders with a couple of other guys who were helping out that were happy just being part of the process. That was day one. Let's fast forward a year.

The school was doing well, but the level of interest, focus, and dedication levels of all four of the partners were diminishing. The cracks were beginning to show as a result of different values.

We had so many meetings it was ridiculous. All they were was a place to moan about what each other wasn't doing and what we individually wanted.

During this time, only two of the guys were teaching full-time for the school. I wasn't one of them. However, my passion and desire to grow was more significant than ever, and I was training as much as I could. Alongside my close protection job, I dedicated myself to developing my business knowledge as quickly as possible, as I realised this was the key to our success..

The relationship between all of the partners severely suffered. It was painfully obvious that things needed to change. One of the partners had a full-time career in the police and was planning on having a family, and so he eventually decided to bow out. A smart choice. A great guy, but as it turns out, he was not a business-driven man.

I believe that if you're going to grow a business successfully, you have to give it all. If you're still working for someone else, your attention, efforts, and focus are split.

I'd like to ask you a question. What do you believe the single most significant thought that holds us back is?

I'll tell you. It's the fear of failure. It's terrifying!

The chance of failure, uncertainty, and ultimately humiliation if it all comes falling down can be debilitating. But that's the risk. Your job is not to let that happen. Commit fully or do not commit at all.

Of course, I don't mean put yourself in financial jeopardy. Decide on a time when you will commit, do it, and never look back. I didn't…

With the police officer out, three of us were left running the school. As they say, two is company; three is a crowd. We were all very committed to the growth of the club, and I thought this was our time to move forward.

Sadly not. Our visions were not aligned, we all kind of wanted to get to the same destination, but we couldn't agree how we were going to get there.

The school was successful. We had an income of over £500,000 and over 600 students. However, that didn't happen without backbreaking work.

"Ah, but Jon" I hear you say, "running a £500,000 business is always going to be hard, whatever you're doing." This is true, but it wasn't the work that was the challenge, the relationship between the three of us felt like we were pulling teeth.

Meetings would always be about trying to solve our disagreements. I spent a lot of my time as 'referee' between the other two guys. I liked both of them, they had been good friends to me, helpful training partners, and outside of work, we had many adventures together. It was certainly not all bad, and I'd never change what we had as friends.

But when it came down to the fundamentals of running and growing the school, the relationship breakdown became very challenging indeed. It started to dramatically affect friendships, something I'd been trying to avoid.

It got the point whereby we decided to agree to a separation. Neil, (the guy who had his own school in the beginning) decided to go at it alone, and Jim and I would continue to work together.

I didn't want this to happen. Neither did I want to be seen to be taking sides. But at the same time, I didn't want the brand to fail. I knew Neil was more than capable of running a school on his own. I was confident he'd have the ability to grow another strong team as he'd done it before. The separation went as well as it could, and Neil went on to build a prosperous school and a new brand with excellent instructors.

He left with a bigger school than he had at the beginning, more experience, and a vision of what he wanted out of life. Neil and I are still good friends to this day. He is a fellow senior instructor in Krav Maga Global UK and is somebody whose friendship I greatly value.

His departure left Jim and I with what we considered a fresh start. We had big plans and ideas and were (I thought) clear on who was going to do what, and how we were going to grow. We needed help to understand how we were going to achieve what we wanted, so we hired a business coach.

As we began to learn from the business coach, I started to read more and implement the learning, yet it soon became apparent that my partner was not doing the same. Getting him to commit to implementation and consistency was a challenge. He seemed to focus so much on the 'here and now', and I preferred long-term planning.

I felt that he depended on me above and beyond our 50/50 partnership. The workload upon me was getting bigger and bigger, and it was not the future I wanted. I was struggling, and no matter how hard I tried I could not seem to communicate the issues. We'd always end up arguing. I believe this was as much my issue as his; we couldn't see eye-to-eye.

All I needed was more help. I needed him to step up more, even if it was a little tricky at times, or meant learning a new skill.

Jim was not a bad guy, he had a massive heart, and would help anyone who asked for it. Everybody liked him. He interacted well with the students, but behind the scenes, he wasn't there. He'd always comment I was not a people person and he was right. But what he didn't realise was that time was so precious, to get everything done that I had very little time to for non-essential conversations and things that didn't matter that much. I'm not a chit-chat kind of guy, but I like purpose in a conversation. This comes down to personalities of course, but I needed to be strict with my time otherwise I'd be working 18 hours a day forever, and that would not have been good for my health.

Jim did the day-to-day things in the business, but that's not what we needed. We needed to both develop and move to a higher level as school owners. He was comfortable doing the smaller, more manageable things that he had a lesser chance of getting wrong. Therefore his responsibility and accountability were less. Making mistakes is part of business and learning.

When we both started out, 50/50 made sense. However, just because that's how it was at the start doesn't mean that's how it will always be. If the structure of the business changes, the reward needs to reflect that. I'm ok with doing more than someone else, but if you do and achieve more, the rewards should be higher. Every business works like this, your job role and responsibilities are recognised by what you get back. It's much like a marriage, if both people do not put the same effort, issues are undoubtedly going to arise.

I was working all day on the phones, handling emails, developing the business and teaching in the evenings. We had a few instructors now (which was a huge learning curve!) I was so committed to our success, I even quit my dream job in the close protection sector.

When my friends and family heard I was quitting, they thought I was mad. In fact, some still think I am. But I know what I wanted, and I was not in charge of my time, something that is far more valuable to me than an excellent salary and travel opportunities. Growing the school was most important to me, and I was willing to commit fully.

In contrast, I found Jim would start tasks and never finish them, or would have ideas but never action them. He'd never work on the important stuff, and any discussion around growth, change, or his attitude to doing more was always met with resentment. At the time, I took this very personally, and it was hard to manage.

He was a good instructor, and I respect him to this day, yet I now know that reluctance to change and move forwards came from our lack of shared vision and destination for the business. What he wanted from the company and where he saw it going was very different to me.

Despite the best efforts of our business coach to get us communicating about these more long-term matters, we never could. Conversations and meetings would always be about small, insignificant things that wasted so much valuable time.

Of course, I was not perfect; I was a challenging guy to work with. I'll admit that. I was not scared to take risks if it meant moving forwards even though sometimes I was not exactly clear on the destination I was travelling to, I just have a lot of faith in positive action, trying new things and seeing what happens.

I'd say the single biggest failure on my part was not understanding that not everybody with the same knowledge will use it in the same way I do. This was a selfish and egotistical attitude, something I have endeavoured to change about myself over the last few years but was a major contributing factor to the relationship breakdown.

This situation continued to escalate until a decision had to be made. We would have split sooner, but values got in the way. I consider myself a loyal person and so I have to be right at the end of a road in either a business or personal relationship to decide to end it. This is both a good thing and a bad thing. It has often prevented me from making the right decision much earlier in many circumstances, both in and out of work. If I was going to decide to split the partnership, then I needed to be entirely sure that it was the right thing do to do. What I needed to know was that if I were unable to work the 18-hour shift I had been, would the business rely solely on me and fall-over? Or would it continue to operate with Jim leading it? Finding this out would help my decision.

Any business that relies solely on you is (I'm afraid) not a business, it's a job. Having a self-sustaining company is a sign of a prosperous one. If can you step away from the company for a period of time and it still runs without you needing to be there you're onto a winner.

Personally, I don't believe in these theories that the business should be able to operate without you entirely, so you can sit back and drink cocktails. That may be the case in some investment scenarios, but if you hold the position as a director or key player, then principally, your input in some way is critical. I'm sure as you are passionate about the business, you would always want that to be the case.

Back to my story, I needed to know what would happen if I wasn't there. Our krav maga governing body, Krav Maga Global (KMG) is based in Israel, it has representation in over 60 countries, and I was quite close with the head instructor, Eyal Yanilov and his General Manager at the time. After many discussions, an opportunity arose whereby I could go and live in Israel for six months, and assist with the growth of the system and KMG. This was an excellent opportunity for me as it would enable:

More experience;

A chance to live and train in Israel and become better in the system I teach by training with Eyal and other masters, like Ze'ev Cohen; and

To see if my school would survive without me.

I discussed this opportunity with Jim, and we both agreed that me going there would be good for our reputation and status as a school, and KMG would welcome any help I could give to grow the system we teach.

At this time, I did not say to Jim that one of my other reasons to go was to find out whether our partnership was long-term or not. This was something I needed to find out for myself, to make sure the decision was right to break the partnership.

After being in Israel for six weeks, frustration started to grow between Jim and I. I was still able to do 90% of my work from Israel, as it was all online, with the exception of teaching, but we had a team of instructors for that. As I suspected, me not being there every day was causing severe issues.

It was clear that without me driving us, the school was not going to move forward. Jim and I needed to split the partnership; our visions just weren't aligned. My mind was made up. I wanted to end the partnership and do so amicably and avoid fighting over the school. That would have been awful for the students. I decided to tell him that I wanted to go our separate ways and we needed to find a way to do that.

The only issue was, I was living in Israel, so I planned to wait until I got back. However, the frustrations got very bad, and I couldn't wait, so I told him that I wanted us to separate. As expected, he didn't take this very well and decided to fly over to Israel to speak with me. When he arrived, I anticipated a huge argument. Surprisingly, we actually got on very well, we talked things through, but my mind was made up. In times of crisis, people can pull through, but it's often short-lived, and people go back to their old ways. Although I was tempted to try again, I stayed strong as knew this was the right decision.

The negotiations around the separation were not easy. My goal was to keep the school as intact as we could, to maintain the excellent teaching standards that we had that was helping so many students progress.

The offers on the table were simple:

I'd keep the school and buy Jim out; or he'd keep the school, and I'd keep the local classes where I lived.

In all honesty, option one is the one I'd have preferred at the time and would have probably been the best for him, but he went for option two.

Money didn't drive me. Even though I'd invested more to keep us afloat through unexpected cash-flow issues. What I cared about was not seeing the school that we had been building for so long, fall down.

I know that he felt that the cash flow issue was the reason for me leaving, but this was never the case. I was willing to take the school on and buy him out and take on the cash flow issue and deal with it myself. But I feel he used this as a reason to justify my decision to split, suggesting I was 'running away', rather than owning up to the fact that our relationship was broken.

I wanted to keep the school. I had a full plan in place should he have chosen option one. It included investing more money back into the business to get it stable and solve the issue by selling my apartment to get some money together for investment. I had a vision of what I wanted to create. I wanted to build the school. I didn't care what I had or didn't have; I was willing to do anything to make it work.

But he wanted option two, and I didn't have the energy to fight. I slowly reduced my work in the school and my financial drawings up to a point whereby I'd sign-over my shares and resign as a director.

I left with a small amount of money in the bank, a small group of students in my local area and the two local instructors who were teaching in that area. I had enough money to pay the instructors for three months, after that, we were in trouble. I'd then either sell my apartment or find a job.

So many people have asked me why I didn't fight more for the school, for the brand, and for money. The only reason I can give is that it no longer represented my vision, we'd have never agreed, and as the negotiations were long and drawn out, I started to fall out of love with the brand.

The school was like a cruise liner that had once sailed the ocean with pride, with a great crew, with everyone having a great time. Somehow it had got stuck in the port. It always needed work doing as it got older and I didn't know how to fix it. Especially with the current set-up. Above all, it was making me very unhappy.

I'm pleased to say that Jim is still running the school in a much smaller capacity. I'm glad he kept it going, and dealt with the restructuring of the business in his own way. Hopefully, now it's fulfilling his vision.

I very much doubt that Jim still sees me as a friend. When things end, they generally end badly, or they don't end at all. If we ever run into each other, the past is the past, it does not shape the future, and I'd always be glad to have a coffee with him. I doubt that will ever happen.

I learnt a lot from this period about growing krav maga schools, but it was time to move on. I walked away from a 500k business, and I have never looked back.

Could I have taken the business on and made it enjoyable again? Absolutely, I was ready to do that, but he was adamant he wanted to keep it. I'm glad he did. What I did next would become the school I had set out to build to give me the life I want.

I had to build almost from scratch, and I needed to grow fast. That meant finding help.

CHAPTER CHECKPOINTS

How much time do you invest on personal development?

Do you invest as much in business training as you do in krav maga training?

What is your perspective towards failure?

Chapter nine

Everybody loves Raymond.

*"Investing in yourself is the fastest way
to grow to where you want to be"*

Walking away from a 500k business was not an easy decision. It took me a long time to pluck up the courage to do it. Of course, I made a point of consulting people I thought could give me a balanced view.

Choosing the right people in life to ask advice and guidance from is often not as easy as it sounds. Many people struggle with the skill of actually listening when you ask for their advice, and many will always somehow make your issue or challenge about them, rather than considering your position. This is not helpful. In some cases, paying for expert guidance, coaching, or mentoring is a much better route to gain the opinions that you need to make major, life-changing decisions.

If I was going to build a new school fast, I'd need some help. So I contacted our old business coach Ray and said I wanted to work with him in developing my new school and I'd find a way to afford it.

Much like any form of coach, trainer, or instructor, my advice to you is to choose wisely. The most important thing is that you must get on with them as people, but more than that, the best choice is someone who is a different character trait that you. I'm fast paced, a little bit full on shall we say. Ray is quiet, slows things down, and thinks everything through; we were the perfect match. I know what you're thinking, if Ray was going to help me build my krav maga school, he must have grown one himself right? Wrong.

Ray is an unassuming character, a highly detailed individual with a lot of knowledge and experience about a variety of businesses. He was initially part of a business coaching franchise, yet soon decided that he wanted to go his own way. He adapted the models he'd been using and introduced new ones based on his experience.

Business coaching can often be confused with mentoring. I define mentoring as being led by someone in the same field as you, who has a proven method for growth and success and you're following that model. A mentor is only likely to work with people in the same industry as they are involved with. They won't tell you what to do specifically, but they will show you proven strategies you can apply as necessary to fit your structure. Some people are both mentors and coaches, but I think keeping a clear definition between the two helps you work out what you need.

A business coach is more like the football manager who didn't play in the Premier League, but they know the game, they've studied the game, they know it inside out, and have worked with 1000's of footballers.

They've seen the classic mistakes, they've seen the roaring successes, and they have intelligently worked out the common denominators in both and can relate these learnings to any business.

Let's be clear on something. No business is unique. Regardless of what you do, the underlying model remains the same. Most struggling school owners use the excuse that their company or school is not growing because it's a different model. Sorry. It's not! Irrelevant of its business activity, every company has the same needs. It requires sales processes, financial management, capable teams, organisational structures, and a guideline for their daily activities.

Every business coach has their strengths and weaknesses, much like personal fitness trainers. Some are good are building your strength, others are better at helping you improve your running time. Ray excelled in the subjects of financial management, leadership, company structures, and above all, personal development. Supporting the business owner become a better person so they can make better decisions, live life more in-line with their values and see their business as a vehicle to help them achieve what they want to in life.

I also trusted what he had to say and valued his opinion. A critical factor when choosing a coach. I've heard of some awful business coaches who will say absolutely anything. My friend Steve is a perfect example. His coach told him: "Steve, your personality traits are the same as most of the top billionaires in the world."

If a business coach had ever said that to me, they might well have experienced some of my krav maga training first hand. What a load of rubbish. Saying that to someone is not helpful. I've known Steve for years. He does not have those traits. He is a fantastic person and dedicated to what he does, but that information was incorrect, and just used to motivate him. Then, when he doesn't do as well as the billionaires of this world, how is that going to affect his dreams and aspirations?

Ray was not like this, his company ethos was "the coaching practice of choice". He put the client first, which in my opinion, is an exceptional approach.

I was not the easiest of clients. Ex-Military, who had travelled the world with one of the world's wealthiest people and seen a lot. I also thought I was smart. I may have seen a few places and know some stuff, but the first thing I realised was that my level of emotional intelligence was low.

Many people have a high IQ. They are strong in the areas of maths, logic, verbal reasoning, many of the academic strengths. But they lack emotional intelligence: the ability to relate and interact with others.

If someone was to ask me the single, most critical thing I learnt from having a business coach, it's how important emotional intelligence is. It's also about how it can shape the way you make decisions and limit conflict in your life.

Separate to running the school, I now teach a corporate conflict communication programme written by conflict expert and author of Meditations on Violence: Rory Miller. At the time of writing, I'm one of only four people in the world certified to teach this course. It's a course about how conflict occurs, from the routes of our evolution to modern times, and how to de-escalate it. More importantly, you learn how to become actively aware of your emotional state. It pays to be aware of it as this is highly likely to be the reason your school is not going in the direction you would like and feels stuck.

To improve your emotional intelligence, you need to be open to the understanding that everything you do and say is rarely conscious, and that most decisions you make are not about solving the problem, they are about maintaining your status. If you want to read more on this subject, I highly recommend Rory's booked Conflict Communication, or another great read is The Chimp Paradox by Prof Steve Peters.

I've worked with Ray for a long time now, and if I'm truly honest with myself, as I write this book I can say that only now am I beginning to implement his teachings. You might ask why if I've had coaching for so long, are things only happening now?

Sometimes you learn things, yet do not fully understand them and therefore are not ready to implement them. Things take time to build, and often you go through challenges and experiences and realise, had you applied a particular piece of advice or knowledge, the problem may not have occurred, or the result may have been different. But you need that challenge to realise this. I know that sounds strange, but if you don't understand something, how can you control it, or limit the impact? Hence the expression, learning from our mistakes.

John Kavanagh, the coach of MMA Champion Conor McGregor, entitled his book: Win or Learn. I believe the title is sound advice both in training and business. Either you're winning and hitting your goals, or you're learning. I do not believe in failure, I believe in results.

You do something, there is a result, is that in-line with what you planned it to be? Or was it a different result? If so, what are the factors that affected the outcome not being as expected? Was it lack of information, lack of clarity? Unrealistic goals being set based on a lack of resources and knowledge. Either way, there is always a lesson to be learnt.

Ray also taught me the meaning of values, to understand that to live a peaceful life, in-line with what you want, is all about knowing, understanding and living by your values. Sometimes this does involve being honest with yourself about who you are, rather than who you would like to be or, more importantly, who you would like others to think you are. We are almost always affected by the fear of what people think of us. We stop doing things in a certain way or changing stories or truths just to save face in front of a group of people we believe care. Trust me, they don't… they've got their own stuff going on.

We learn best through models, simplistic ways to remember and follow processes, to limit unforeseen consequences. Ray taught me several to help in all aspects of the business. Everything from effective leadership to prioritising, and being as productive as possible.

What I learnt from Ray about this has killed some fears I had around money and finance. By teaching me how to accurately plan my business finances and read a set of accounts I was better equipped to make smarter financial decisions.

I was a krav maga instructor, and that's great. It's where I've come from, yet if I wanted to achieve my dream of living and working with what I enjoyed, and spending each day as I choose, then I had to start to think differently.

If you see people doing things in a certain way and inevitable results they didn't want, but they keep doing the same thing regardless, chances are they are not great people to follow.

The majority of krav maga school owners I meet always wanted the same thing. More students or to be appreciated for how good they are by earning more money or respect. They would also complain that students were not staying long, therefore did not appreciate the training. I have also met, and I spent time with some very successful school owners. But when I say that, I also need to caveat that with what I define as successful, which has absolutely nothing to do with lots of members or money.

Success is what you want it to be. I love hanging around with school owners and instructors who own, work, and grow schools in-line with their goals. Not everyone wants a big school, and if that's the plan and you've kept it small for your own reasons, then that in itself is a success.

If you wanted to grow to have 20 expert levels and you now have taught 20 people up to expert level, you've achieved your own definition of success.

The problem is that people are not clear with what they want, and by clear, I mean absolutely 100% crystal. It can't be some half-baked "I wish" statement. It has to be a very logical, clear, realistic vision that you want to achieve, in a specific time frame.

Why do people struggle with this? Because they want everything. And they feel that if they commit to one thing or two or three specific things, they will miss out somewhere else. So instead they just see what happens. That's a pretty bad strategy.

The age-old theory that krav maga school owners are just part-time instructors doing it as a hobby is gone. Live with it. If you tell yourself that krav maga is just something extra that you do, but deep down you really want to do it full-time, then you're lying to yourself.

Stop it. There are many full-time school owners, and there is no reason why you cannot be one of them if that's your dream.

Running a krav maga school is a full-time vocation, a skill, don't let anybody else tell you otherwise. Anyone who questions whether or not it's real job, probably defines one of those as spending 8-hours a day doing something they hate, working alongside people they don't get on with. Typically a 'real' job is one that (and I hate this phrase) "pays the bills".

I will repeat what I said earlier: life is not a dress rehearsal. You will not lay on your deathbed saying, "well at least I paid all my bills." In fact, I'd probably guess that you'll still have bills outstanding when the big man in the sky tells you it's your turn to head on up!

Do what you love, share your passion with people who love the same thing to, and work with people who teach you how to be better. I still work with Ray to this day. However, he has semi-retired and works with me on the financial management of my school. Business coaching changed my life more than I realised at the time. I will be forever grateful to Ray for his advice, guidance and overall ability to adjust his communication style to help me understand his rationale. Especially when I walked away from my former school, and I did not have a lot of money to pay for his help.

My advice to you is to find a business coach. One that suits your needs. Much like people pay you to coach them in krav maga, find someone who can coach you in the skill of growing a business. Spend some time finding the right person. As the same in your own loving relationships, you need to find out if the person is right for you. After all, you're going to spend a lot of time together, share some very personal stories and challenges and you're going to pay for the privilege. Use this person to your advantage, truly listen, implement what they say and trust me, the journey you're on will be far more enjoyable, and you will rise above the rest.

If financing a business coach would be tight for you right now, start to talk with and spend time with successful school owners. Many will be happy to offer advice over a coffee. Being around the right people is essential to the success of your school. Spend time with them, ask meaningful questions, and listen. Be sure to implement their advice and test the results. You might be surprised!

CHAPTER CHECKPOINTS

How do you practise active listening?

How do you keep yourself accountable?

What are your strengths and weaknesses in business?

Chapter ten

Tried and tested.

*"Your fears are not unique, seek out those
who've pushed through to the other side"*

There is a saying that if you're the smartest person in the room, then you're in the wrong one. I like spending time with like-minded people that are better than me on some level. To do that I always make an effort to be part of a Mastermind group or go to a business development seminar every few months. Rubbing shoulders with successful individuals at these events will give you a gentle nudge in the right direction towards your goals. For one thing, you can learn from the mistakes of others without the negative fallback on your own school.

Many of these workshops, courses, and seminars have guest speakers on stage. Often, listening to them will trigger lightbulb moments, or, a BFO: a blinding flash of the obvious. This is when you realise you have been doing something a certain way, yet there was a much easier way to do it. These BFO's will save you a lot of energy and be kinder to your cash flow. Or, they'll be the solution you've been looking for with a particular struggle that you're having.

If you decide to attend a business seminar, beware that you do not become what is known as a seminar junkie. I've lost count the number of times this has happened to me at various events, I always go back with a notebook full of ideas, which of course need the time to be implemented.

Try and avoid falling for marketing tactics. These typically are that you're going to miss out due to limited space. By all means, if it suits you, sign up to the next event but make sure you have time to take stock of what you've just learnt and implemented the processes in your own school and taking action.

My friend James defines the difference between motion and action exceptionally well.

Motion is floating from place to place, making notes, having ideas and big thinking sessions, yet never translating into anything actionable. Nothing gets done, and you don't move forward.

Action is taking what you learn and applying it to your everyday business activities.

The world famous info-marketer Dan Kennedy makes a joke about people going to his (huge!) live events where he sees people taking pictures of his presentation slides with their phone and making pages and pages of notes. He says people will never use them, so better to take ten notes and action all of them, rather than 100 and action none. So true!

These types of events can either be generic for business, or specific to martial arts. Events that focus on your particular field are the best. You'll be hanging around with people who think similarly to you or at least understand your language.

If you choose to go to a specific martial arts business event, try to steer away from school owners that get stuck in conversations about techniques and whose style is best.

This is not helpful and is mostly a waste of time in these types of forums. Leave it for the mat. You might think you're discussing coaching principles to improve your club members, but this is not the place. It kills your energy having those chats, as no one is ever right, and you'll lose focus.

There is one public speaker who always stood out. I was always very impressed with his energy and enthusiasm for growing schools.

His name is Allie Alberigo. He is a lifelong martial artist and has grown a very successful business from it. To top it off, he's a Ninja.

At this point, I can't help but quote my favourite Ninja joke…

"I'm a Ninja!"

"No, you're not!"

"Did you see me do that?"

"Do what?"

"Exactly!"

Don't groan. I know you loved it.

His tremendous success in the martial arts industry has led Allie to become a mentor for many successful school owners. At the height of his career, he had schools all over the world, located in Puerto Rico, Costa Rica, Bermuda, Upstate New York, and five schools on Long Island, plus an array of associate schools. His monthly financial income was a staggering $200,000 per month, with over 2000 students.

After the birth of his daughter, Kiara, Allie decided to take a new direction and simplified his business operations and reduced his travel schedule, as he was teaching nine months of the year travelling around the world. He made a point of visiting all of his local schools regularly; it was an excellent leadership quality, but not very healthy for his family life.

To create more of a balance, Allie decided to cut back and level out his work load. He sold a number of his schools or gifted them to their head instructors and moved to help others grow their martial arts schools through mentorship.

Allie still operates two schools on Long Island. One in Boynton Beach Florida and a small private school in New York serving a particular group of members.

I got on very well with Allie. I still work with him from time to time when I decide to take my school to the next level. If I ever run a krav maga success seminar or workshop, you can be assured that Allie will be one of those people who'll be speaking at that event. Don't miss out; he's a goldmine of knowledge.

Allie taught me a lot about my brand and what it represented. How I needed to paint a particular message to the world. We also looked at the types of images that krav maga schools use to promote themselves poorly. When I look around at other schools, I see these mistakes repeatedly. Typically it's because each school copies others marketing and branding. Sadly they do so with no idea if it works or not. They assume if others do it it must be good. Right? On the contrary.

Allie also helped me to understand the goal of my online presence. My website and about the new student experience. One thing was evident, and that's it didn't matter how good I was at krav maga. If the experience of booking their first class on my website was challenging, potential new students will get frustrated and click off my site. This type of information gave me the motivation to learn more about web marketing, online customer experience, and student relationships, both on and off the training floor.

One of the most important lessons I learnt was to give people the best experience possible. If a life-long martial artist wanted to join my school, we already speak the same language, and they'd confidently jump right into training. But these people are few and far between. I shouldn't direct my advertising to these people. They don't need convincing; they'll come anyway.

I believe that most people who want to start krav maga training never actually do it. They look at your website and videos numerous times, yet stay sitting on the sofa because there is not enough information and interaction between you and them BEFORE you meet them, the exposures they need to help them gain the confidence to show up to class and try it out.

Turning up is the hardest part. Arriving at a new place, surrounded by new people, to do something that you've never done before. Especially in krav maga; an activity that involves physical contact. One that goes against their basic instincts. Think about it. People have been told the same rules all their lives: "Don't hit your sister." "Don't hit your brother." "Don't be rude to people." "Be nice." That's how your students have been raised — now you're teaching them that kicking and punching are ok in certain situations.

That's a hard change to cope with for many people and very overwhelming, but as instructors, we take it for granted. One of the most significant learning points as a career krav maga instructor and school owner is that I realised I'm an addict. And you are too. Yes look in the mirror, an addict is staring back at you.

You are not normal. You're addicted to krav maga. You love it. You always think about it, you practice it, and you run a business in it. Everybody else is 'normal.' They do it now and again. They might start for a while and stop.

Your role is to appreciate this and to help them make a behavioural change, to stay the course and not quit. Of course, you will get a few who will become addicted, but most will remain enthusiastic amateurs, and that's fine. Keep them excited through giving them a fantastic experience both on and off the mats. So much so, krav maga forms an integral part of their busy lives. Make it something they cannot live without. If they miss it, they crave it.

Allie helped me create this experience, from the initial contact to the meet and greet to being on the mats, and dealing with ongoing challenges. Where did Allie learn what works and what doesn't? By trying and testing it himself, in his own business. Making the mistakes and celebrating the wins.

I now give various presentations about growing krav maga schools. These cover business, coaching skills, and of course krav maga training to multiple instructors within our network and across the world. From experience, there is nothing more frustrating than presenting to a group and being met with: "Well that will never work."

How can you possibly know if something will work or not unless you test it? You can't. People are afraid of achieving. They are scared of the unknown and what they might find out.

To be honest, I was the same. Nevertheless, Allie showed me that growing a school was a combination of using his advice, but also testing out my own theories and ideas, to find out what works best, and that means taking a few risks.

How can you actually fail at something? After testing a theory, you have a result, and that result is information that you use to change the way you do it next time. One of the biggest mistakes a school owner can make is refusing to part with money to educate themselves. This is not advisable. You need to invest time and money into new ideas and new concepts to grow. So long as it's well applied and you can track the results, these methods will propel your school forward.

If the way you operate currently is not getting you the results you want, change it.

There is a classic phrase by Einstein: "The definition of insanity is doing the same thing over and over again, but expecting different results." You can brush over that quote, but you cannot ignore its validity.

"Ah but Jon, I don't know what to test and what to try?" I don't entirely believe this for a second. I have sat with many school owners who know precisely where the problems are in their schools. Fixing them or trying new things means taking some risks; ones they avoid it at all costs. The classic phrase when talking about new ideas, or problems to fix is "Yeah, I know"… well if you know, why don't you change it?

Within my team, I now have a very open approach to trying new ideas, processes, and concepts in the effort to grow and improve. If one of your team (instructors or students) presents a plan, they deserve for you to give them the time to listen. If logically it could work and doesn't show any imminent risks, why not let them explore it and see how it goes?

Of course, set parameters and monitor the process, but this is how you will get the best out of people. Give them opportunities to grow, shine, and succeed. We live in a world where we are told "no" so often. Why not push yourself and see what happens when you say "yes" every once in a while?

If one of my team presents an idea, and they have mapped out all the what if's, reasons and potential improvements, I will always let them run with it. If it doesn't go to plan, so what? Did they learn something? Did they become a better person through that experience? Absolutely! It's good to remember; you do not know everything. That's why we hire people better than ourselves.

When you become open to everything. The world becomes a much more exciting place, and you end up getting what you want. How do I know? It's working for me right now.

Think about the things you know you need to change that will have a massive impact on your school. Why are you avoiding this? If it's fear, you need to talk it through with someone. Find a coach or a mentor who will give you sound advice based on what the information you present to them. It's often the kick you need to take action.

Stop over analysing everything. Go and make some changes. More importantly, enjoy the results that come out of it.

CHAPTER CHECKPOINTS

Are you a person of motion or of action?

What image does your krav maga school present?

What is your 'new student experience' process?

Chapter eleven

Snake oil.

*"Your website is like the path to your house. If
you don't cut the grass, it will get overgrown.
Nobody will be able to find your front door."*

When taking advice and guidance from others, it's a good idea to
look to consultants or experts in their chosen fields. For me, this was
Brad (who you met earlier), director of Sixth Division.

Brad created the six laws of implementation. The things in business
you need to do well to get things done. I won't go through them all
but there is one law which has always stuck with me, and that's:
"You are not a plumber."

If you have a problem with the water system or the pipes in
your house, you rarely spend hours trying to fix it yourself. It's too
important. DIY attempts are expensive and more often than not
end up being a disaster, and so you get a specialist in. You call a
plumber.

Even though you might pay that specialist a fee, you'll save time.
You'll get a better result and reduce the chances of having to fix the
problem again.

The same goes for areas of your krav maga school. The most
significant and most important task is having your website built. If
there's anything you take from this book, it's that you get it done by
a professional. This is critically important.

Imagine your site as a high street shop. It must look appealing and
attract attention from passersby. Above all, people need to be able
to find your shop. Your website must function in the same way. Your
krav maga school must be visible online, and if that means paying a

little bit more to be on the internet high street, or as we call it, the 'front page of Google', then so be it.

Copying a website, or putting something together yourself using a do it yourself programme might seem to save you a little bit of money now, but the detrimental long-term effects are not worth the saving. Plagiarism is NOT the way forward. It will not help you reach your goals, and it can open you up to being sued.

If you want a presence on Google, you need an expert to design your website and write your content. There are many to choose from, but you must take the same approach as when buying a car. Do your research and be careful who you're giving your money too. Make sure they do what they say they will.

One of the things I ensure is that I know a little about a lot of things. I'm not a website expert, but I've researched what makes a successful website. When I'm talking to an expert, it helps me ask the right questions. The same goes for other areas of your business.

For example, knowing the basics of:

- Accounting;
- Leasing property;
- Filming great videos;
- CRM software; and
- Web design and online marketing

Will help you substantially along your journey.

There's a method behind the madness of learning the basics myself. It's so when I visit various web designers I don't get sold the snake oil of web designing. You know the one. The mystical lotion, a secret solution, that I don't know anything about. But I'm assured that when I rub it into my skin, it will make me look 21 again. It's just going to cost that little bit more than regular products. You get my point.

Many web designers have a habit of not speaking your language. They will baffle you with various methods of SEO and other techniques that help you achieve faster growth on Google. This is the exact definition of snake oil! It sounds impressive, but you don't understand it, and therefore are relying on the authority of the web designer and their magical lotions to make you 21 again.

What do you look for in a web agency?

Find an agency with proven happy clients. One that communicates with you (you'd be surprised how many web teams seem to fall into the Bermuda Triangle 6 days a week!) Find a separate branding team and content writer. You might think this sounds expensive but with a few conversations with genuine agencies; you'll see this is not the case.

It's important to know there are three aspects to a website. The technical stuff, the way it looks, and what is on there. For that, you need three different people. You wouldn't ask your plumber to fix your electrics and lay your new floorboards.

Something else to consider is, are you impressed by their website? If someone tries to sell me web services, the first thing I'm going to do is check the site of their company. Can I find them easily? Is their website clear? Does it make me want to read more? Are their services explained in plain English, or is it all written in snake oil. Designed to dupe me into needing ALL of the extra services.

The second criteria is that they understand web marketing, not just design.

It's all about the customer.

Web design and web marketing are not the same. I want to know that the company I'm going to work with understand the 'customer journey'.

If you go in to a shop, and you can't find what you specifically want, or if there is no one to ask questions to and it becomes frustrating then, unless I absolutely need the product (which means no selling process is involved) then I'm just going to leave.

Your website must be the same. The customer journey must be impeccable. It must be clear what you do, where you do it, and how to start and find out more, by speaking to a human or receiving some additional information via email in a simple way.

I have lost count of the amount of krav maga school owners who ask me to review their website, and when I check the site out, I usually get confused as it lists everything that they could do. There are always lists of courses they run or seminars that they are going to hold, and that confuses me.

If I'm a potential new student, then these things are not relevant to me. I just want more information and learn how to start training. Do not confuse your website as a portal for both existing and new students, they both have very different needs. Have you ever looked at the site of your bank? They always have a separate route for new customers and existing customers ones, so you only see the information that's relevant to you. The way you communicate with existing members is different. They are already in your circle. You have their details, and you can send them to a separate web page, website, or use various social media groups. In the words of Ghostbusters, "don't cross the streams."

Your website must have a one clear and simple goal, and all routes on your site must drive towards that goal. Visitors will do one of three things:

Look to book a class;

Find your details to contact you; and

Leave the site, having done nothing.

Based on behaviours around fear and trust the majority will leave your website and look elsewhere. If you allow people to do this, it's like letting customers walk into your shop without offering them more advice about your products and services.

You need to add a fourth option!

There MUST be something on your website that can be downloaded, or watched in return for their contact information, so you can, with their permission, (this is called opting-on and has strict rules) send them further information to help them decide whether your school is right for them or not.

The information must be of true value. It must share an experience that can be related to, or teach something that can be understood. It must be usable and would make the person keen to learn more.

Once you send them that information, there must be a clear option to unsubscribe if they choose they do not want to know more. Somebody opting in for more information and them unsubscribing is not a bad thing, it means they were not the right person for your school. If they do not unsubscribe, then begin a process of building a relationship with them, so they feel comfortable finding out more, potentially coming to class, or booking an introductory course.

People only buy from a business that they know, like, and trust. This is the golden rule in marketing. People do not buy from random strangers; they must connect in some way with you and your school. First impressions are everything, and a quality website will position your school as highly desirable. Much like a first date, it takes time for you know them. At which point the relationship may then progress.

Just asking people to book a class there and then with no other option is much like asking everyone to marry you on the first date. It's unlikely to happen!

Before asking a potential new member for their hand in marriage, it's probably a good idea to find out as much about them as you can, to make sure that they are going to be a good fit for you, and to give you a fighting chance at a long-lasting relationship. You need to know what they are looking to achieve, what their goals are, and if they have any concerns. This can be done through an online survey, an email with questions, or through a phone call.

You want to find out the real reason why somebody is looking to come to your school. Almost all of the time they have an issue they wish to resolve. Of course, you do have a large batch of impulse buyers who are not clear on why it might just have looked cool. These people still, deep down, have things they want to achieve. It's your job to find out what and extract what these things are and associate your krav maga school as part of their solution, and to present the gains they'll achieve.

To manage your expectations and make your contact appropriate, it's a good idea to gauge your new contacts level of interest. Are they serious about joining right now? Or are they just asking the right questions to gather information for the future? We call this their level of readiness. There is nothing worse than spending your time explaining what you're doing and how you can help someone, only to then find out that they are moving away next month, changing jobs, or getting married soon and they can't commit to training.

Imagine in the dating world you spend all evening talking to the man or women of your dreams only to find out they are about to go travelling for six months. That's not to say they aren't a potential life partner, yet any progress on that relationship is going to be slowed down considerably. They will still be of interest, but not right now.

That doesn't mean you don't keep in contact with the potential student who after all, shows a commitment that you're thinking about them and you realise they will be back soon.

Being able to talk to someone and clearly show you understand what they are looking to achieve goes a long way to growing a school full of long-term, dedicated members.

Could you sign up all the impulse buyers? You know the ones. The ones that will sign up because of a great special offer. Of course you can, that's easy.

However, the life-span of these members will be short, as they begin this new activity without clear goals aligned with their needs, and in time, the interest fades, the adrenaline buzz wears off, and they go looking for something else.

When you meet the person of your dreams, you know little about them, you start dating, and then it gets a bit real, the falling in love feeling wears off and often one or the other goes looking for the next buzz. No time was spent establishing why the relationship started in the first place and working out ways of making sure it's going well were never thought about.

Start with a long-term view in mind. Build relationships with your prospective members. Find out more about them, actively listen to their stories and then ethically show how what you do can help them, can provide a purpose and that you'll take time to make sure they are progressing.

It all begins with starting to get to know someone, then you'll like them, and then you will trust them. Do not break the trust once it's there, do what you say you're going to do, and people will stay with you for a long time.

There may be the case that your school is not right for the potential new student, so you need to be honest about that. Do not sell snow to the Eskimo. Be clear if something is not right, they will appreciate it later down the line.

There are two types of potential new members that you can encounter. The first is those who find you because they were looking for exactly what you offer, or something very similar.

For example, someone who comes to your classes might have been looking for krav maga, or self-defence in general. Either way, they have an idea of what they are looking to do. These types of people will usually find you through an internet search in their local area. This is where your web design comes in to play as your website should be optimised through SEO for the search terms that people are typing in google. For example, if somebody types in 'krav maga classes in London' it would be inexcusable for me not to be in position one or two in an organic (not paid for) search.

If there is a lot of competition in your area for the same, or similar type of training, then you may well invest in paid online advertising to ensure your school appears at the top of Google. This is called bidding and is almost considered educated gambling. How much are you willing to spend per click to appear above your competition, and that all comes down to how much each new member is worth to you.

The process of paying for Google Adwords can be one (but not the only) marketing tactic you use to let people know you're around. Without getting into the intricate details of Adwords, make sure you control your spend, be clear on the results and understand your financial return on each new member. I know many clubs who have run wild with Google Advertising without control and without tracking results, and they've lost a lot of money during the process. Be careful! Make sure that your chosen web team are clear on your goals, track the results and advise you on where your money is best spent. If they are not sending you a monthly report, and meeting with you regularly about how your website and marketing investments are performing, this should be a concern.

There must be a balance between being found organically and your Adwords campaigns. If your brand becomes strong enough, your ad spends may reduce as more leads come through to you from recommendation and people being more generally aware of what you do. Then you could focus on your SEO which is all about generating the right content on your website.

I'm not suggesting I'm an SEO or Adwords specialist. I know the basics, but I'm not the plumber; I've got someone who's a specialist to help me.

Some people are reading this chapter wondering how on earth they can afford a good web designer and a paid ads specialist. If you start with a little bit of capital, it is not that expensive to get started with decent providers. If you have no budget at all, to get to a point where you can pay for the right people, do the right jobs should be a goal you want to achieve as quickly as possible.

I can pretty much guarantee someone is training in your school who is involved in web design. Speak to them first and it might be that you can arrange an exchange of services deal. Of course, be careful and be clear, structure the right deal for everyone and avoid people doing it as a favour, or for cheaper as they are your friend or student, this never works out well. They will start with good intentions, but it will fade, trust me. By all means, use it as a starting point, but it's not your forever strategy. Get the right people doing the right things, and you will see fantastic results.

My current web team are always tracking our results and reporting our progress. They look at what works and what doesn't and are continually helping to improve our brand, customer experience, and are regularly testing different ads, based on what we offer, to various demographics. And that's why I continue to work with and invest in them.

Many school owners get a website built, pay for it, and then leave it and then wonder why they are not getting any new members. Give your site the attention it needs, gets some sound, professional, and valued advice. Once you have your website, then you can tailor your advertising needs towards the type of new student you're looking for.

CHAPTER CHECKPOINTS

When did you last review your website?

have you researched web marketing versus web design?

Have you mapped out you 'new customer journey'?

Chapter twelve

Beware of false prophets who offer false profits.

"Consistency is a posh word for just doing what you must; without question or excuse."

There are two main types of prospects that you'll encounter. Warm prospects, who are potential students who have come across your school and have got in touch. They might have found your school on purpose off the back of a recommendation, or because they were searching for krav maga training on the internet and came across your site. These are people already open-minded to what you do, therefore would be more open to conversations about membership, prices, and long-term training.

The second type is the person who happens to walk past your school, sees a class going, or maybe they see one of your offers that catches their attention from one of your flyers or posters. In the marketing world, this is called cold traffic.

The way you engage with cold traffic is very different to that of warm traffic. Warm leads already have an idea about what you do, they may have done their own research, or be familiar with krav maga, self-defence, or other forms of martial arts training.

Cold traffic prospects may have been looking for a new activity to start, to reach a broader goal, for example to, get fit, and your advert popped up, or they walked passed your class and thought it looked interesting as they peered through the window.

Social media platforms, such as Facebook, are hunting ground for cold traffic prospects. You can target your advertising to various people who have specific interests, or who are friends with people you or your school are associated with. The message on these adverts needs to be very different.

For example, a warm traffic advert might say: "come and learn krav maga in London at the UK's No.1 school." Whereas an advert for cold traffic might say: "Who else wants to get fit and learn to defend their loved ones while learning something new?"

The first advert suggests that the person looking at it knows what krav maga is. The second advert poses a question about two broader goals, fitness and family safety. It also suggests you have the answer. Then when they click through to your web page, where they will then find out what krav maga is and how that can help them achieve those broader goals.

Of course, you can learn to run some Facebook Ads yourself. Setting them up is pretty straightforward. To understand how to best target your prospects, to know how the wording on your ads makes all the difference, and how the need to split test (this means to compare various ads with minor changes) works is slightly more difficult. Remember you're not the plumber. Therefore either working with a social media specialist from the beginning or taking a training course either in-person or online to get started is hugely valuable. Invest in yourself or better still, a member of your team.

I must offer you this warning from my experience. There is a new breed of expert on the internet, that must be approached with caution should you be looking to outsource your social media marketing or gain some training in what works best.

With the growth of online advertising, the amount of internet millionaires that are popping up is astounding. You can identify them quickly, as they usually promote using a video of them in a sunny climate sitting around a pool, with an expensive car in the background. The story will start with how they went from being broke to a seven-figure income by growing their business online, and you can learn their proven strategy to do the same.

Now, I will not blanket punish here; there are many successful online experts that I have learnt a lot from. The difference is that many of them have proven their models and strategies on real businesses.

A good example is Ryan Deiss from Digital Marketer. They provide various courses and information about growing your business online, yet they have tried and tested their concepts on real companies from survival websites to home DIY products and many more.

Beware of the false prophet, who says they made their first million profit online using a secret strategy to get them 200,000 subscribers on their YouTube Channel, or 1000's of leads to their website through Facebook. Then you ask them what their business does that they got 200,000 subscribers and 1000's of leads to their website. And they answer that their business is…Yes, you guessed it… teaching people how to get 200,000 subscribers and 1000's of leads. So, in fact, YOU became one of those leads, and the method they are using to get you to visit is the method they will teach you. Very smart, but doesn't sit well with me. Trust me, I've fallen for it myself, and I've been taken in by a few of these guru's.

To me this is 100% snake oil, they don't have a real, tangible business that offers a product or service that has proven their model works across various industries.

Some of the experts suggest offering ways in which you can make money by selling other people's products by laying on a beach with your laptop. I'm sure it's possible, but that's not a business in my view. It's merely a way to be an introducer to generate more money. Business means so much more than just an income. So is your krav maga school.

Beware of where you spend your money and on what courses you attend. You choose wisely where to spend your money to learn krav maga; follow the same principles with the learning of the other aspects of your business. Only seek out those who are genuine; like you would with your own krav maga training.

Marketing as a concept is about investment. For every new student that you want to come through the door of your school, there is a cost associated with that new student. You cannot get away from that. You must have an open attitude to investing in marketing. Therefore you must apportion a percentage of your income to reinvest in marketing. Then you need to decide where and how to spend that money making sure to track your results to ensure what you're doing is working for you.

I have met so many krav maga school owners who invest in advertising online, yet without a single piece of information to say whether it's working or not. This is often called hope marketing. As it says on the tin, you hope it will work, and when it doesn't...you blindly continue down the same path.

Much like any other type of investing, such as stocks and shares, you must track your return. As I said before, I'm not an internet marketing genius. It's not my skill set, but I do understand the basics and know what to look for to decide whether I'm getting the results that I want.

If you're not getting the results, there are so many factors that can play a part in this. It could be:

The way you word your marketing.

Your branding.

- The images you use.
- Unappealing and irrelevant offers.
- You're targeting the wrong clients.
- You're not offering enough information.
- You're not giving a clear way for customers to take action.

And let's not discount the old school ways such as flyers, posters, referral cards and any other types of printed material. The chances are that you're already advertising on Facebook or similar platforms. The question to ask yourself is, do you have a strategy? Or are you (much like most websites) copying what others are doing without knowing if it's working or not?

I'm not here to teach you how to build the perfect advert for your school. At this stage, that would not be helpful. Learning how to think is more important.

Nor am I telling you how to develop a marketing strategy. I want to open your mind to the fact you do need to have one. And there are plenty of affordable options available to you.

Online marketing is also about consistency. Be that through adverts, blogging, or producing videos. If you're doing some of this then great. Fix what you have before you start adding to the pile. Evaluate your strategy. See what tools you can use to start tracking your progress. If you're doing it yourself, find a specialist. If you have one, are they running regular reports? If you're doing none of it, that needs to change today.

Small positive steps in the right direction and simply getting started is a massive action step, and for that, I applaud you. Welcoming change, investing in learning and developing is very challenging for your emotional brain. Right now, you know where you sit, you know where you stand, you might not like it. You might want more. But often we are put off through the fear of failure or in fact, the fear of success.

When you start to take action, change happens, sometimes for the better sometimes for worse but either way, it's changing, and we don't like change, so we find reasons to stay where we are. In other words, we embrace the gentle warmth and comfort that procrastination brings. Whatever you do, you must fight this feeling. Learn to adapt to change. With some dedication and focus, I can assure you the difference will be positive.

I could dedicate a whole book to the actual adverts we run, the blogs we write, the videos we make, and how we operate online. But that's not helpful if your mindset is not in the right place, it will just confuse you as to what you should be doing. Plus what works for me, doesn't mean it works for you. You have your own profile of client. You're in a different area. You have a different teaching style. You need the strategy that's going to work for you. One that fits parallel with your why; your goals, and your focus. Once you uncover these, then you can start to work on the how.

Many school owners do this in the wrong order then wonder why they suffer from disappointing results.

CHAPTER CHECKPOINTS

Do you attract both warm and cold traffic?

In what areas of your school are you still a 'plumber'?

Do you think of marketing as an investment or as an expense?

Chapter thirteen

Great expectations.

*"Your list of certificates does not attract
new students. Your attitude does."*

Window shopping is a favourite pastime of many. Slowly moving past different shops and trawling through the internet for something that takes their fancy.

Whether they are looking through the window into your school or class, or the window of their internet browser, your potential new student should picture a place of positivity where they could meet a particular need that they have, or solve a problem that they are facing. Either way, they must see your school as a solution.

Your krav maga lessons are sold as a service, and so when trying to attract more clients, you need to appeal to their inner consumer. To do that, you must show potential new students what is in it for them. Something I see a lot of krav maga schools fail to understand.

When you become an instructor, your business stops being about you. Yes, sorry to break that news to you; you're no longer most important. You need to come to terms with this fact right from the start to develop your marketing strategy to be focused on the potential new students; encompassing your marketing to their needs, concerns, and goals.

Telling them how great your school is, how many certificates you have or how hard the training sessions are, will not help you grow.

Over time, we've become a soft species. We shy away from potentially painful experiences. Yes, dedicated martial artists see pain as something you mentally overcome; but most of your new students are not going to have this mindset. They might, in time, with your coaching and guidance. But the most significant proportion of new business is going to come from students who are cautious and don't know what to expect. If you label your classes as tough, miserable, gruelling, and hardcore you're going quite literally scare most of your business away.

When advertising your school, your sole purpose is to set customers expectations of positive experience from the offset. Earn their trust by making it enjoyable for them. An activity they look forward to and want to return again, and again.

From the moment they land on your website, book their first class, to visiting your school for the first time, it is vital that you set yourself apart from other schools. Position yourself as a professional school, who is serious about what you do. Then fit a student experience around that.

Be mindful of making the process effortless. Answer unasked questions where you can. People are busy. They are not going to remember to call or look later. They want an answer now. If they don't find it, they are gone. It's as simple as that.

I'm not talking about the die-hards. The experienced martial artist who now wants to learn krav maga. These people are going to come and find you anyway. They get it. They understand what happens on the mats. These guys and girls will roll around in a dusty old church hall. They are already conditioned to the benefits of martial arts, they are addicted, just like you. These are not the people you're targeting. So in all honesty, get this type of customer out of your mind. You need to switch your focus to everyone else because that is where the growth is.

This reminds me of a conversation I had with an experienced instructor a few years ago. He said to me: "I've seen your advice about how to bring new members into the club, but we are only interested into the toughest people, the ones who want to spar, who want to train hard five times a week".

My reply…"Ah ok, do me a favour then, everyone else you meet, send them to my school."

Fast forward a year, he's complaining about not being able to run his school, as he doesn't have enough members. Funny that!

He is searching for the needles in the haystack, these are people who show up, train, and either stick at it or move to the next martial arts system. They are probably suffering from injuries from years of training and are getting their latest martial arts fix. You may keep them for a while, but these students are not the basis on which to build your long-term strategy. For these people, we created a unique advanced or sparring class. A place where these people can progress to and can mix with their own type, train how they want with the acceptance of others. Don't get me wrong, I'm very much like these types of students, and most likely so are you, we are the few who love tough sparring, throwing each other to the ground, attacking each other with weapons and loving the feeling of getting the submission. We are the few who enjoy the possibility of getting punched in the face… most (quite rightly) do not!

It's good to have this environment but don't make it your primary focus. Create an experience that's not just for you and the other addicts. Do it for the people who are the opposite of you. Those who look at you like you're weird because you're ok with people punching you in the face, and laughing when it happens. Remember that people are socially conditioned to be well-behaved from an early age, to not fight in the school playground; to be pleasant, polite, and never rude. Then suddenly in a krav maga class, they are being asked to do the opposite.

It takes time to break that type of conditioning, for them to realise it's ok to do what they were told not to, in the right place, at the right time and in the right context. Once they break that conditioning it's very liberating for them, their level of competence and skill grows, and when you get good at something, you feel more confident, and that creates better, stronger and more positive human beings. Your job is done!

Creating experiences is about giving people a look inside the depths of your soul, how you and your team can help them, to make them stronger, fitter, and more confident. In turn, this new found mindset will improve many other areas of their life. First impressions count the most. When the new, nervous person visits your website, it should set them on the path of least resistance to contact you or to come and meet you.

Website 101.

Use the following as a checklist to determine whether or not your website does what it needs to:

Strategy and structure. What is your goal, and does the whole site focus towards it? For example, If you're looking for more students, does your site help people to book their first class?

Look and layout. How does it look and how is it laid out in line with the goal, do all pathways lead to the target?

Wording. What wording do you use? Does it make people wonder, feel excited, interested, and curious?

Offers & opt-ins. Are you creating a special, compelling offer that people will want to take up? Are you following the rules of an irresistible offer? Do you have a simple way for people to 'opt-in' for more info and do you follow up with them, both online and offline to talk more about your special offer? For example, running a free intro class or trial class that costs a small amount of money.

Payments and processing. If people book online, is the process of doing so seamless or do they have to 'click' five times to get to where they need to do? How do you communicate that their booking was successful and then start to confirm everything they need to know, to kill that feeling of uncertainty? People like to know everything as early as possible, and not to have to worry about what they will need, what to expect and what will happen.

Mistakes and mysteries. Are you aware of the biggest mistakes that krav maga schools make when building a website? Do you know why some perform well and others don't? Have you done your research? Did you copy a website design without knowing if it works well or not? Have you asked somebody more experienced than you to review your website?

As you can see, each of these areas are for a more extensive discussion, but ultimately, they represent the start of the experience you are creating.

Your website is your shop window; are people walking in or skirting past?

If I use my website as an example, I usually get two types of feedback.

"Your website was easy to use, I love the way to get all the information quickly so I can plan."

"I got too many emails from you about my trial class and what your club is about."

Both of these types of feedback are good. It has nothing to do with what we send. More so, the personality of the recipient.

Type one is a planner, someone who loves info, confirmation and knowing all the details so they can plan and prepare, this is most people who start something new.

Type two is more about running day-to-day, doesn't like a lot of info and will be where they need to be and will roll up somehow on the day and probably have done a similar activity.

Either way, the fact I got a response from both types is a win! I can then respond appropriately.

"That's great, anything else you need to know, drop us a line!" or; "I know it's a lot sometimes it's just we are a popular school. I'm sure you can imagine not everyone is as well organised as you, so we are just making sure no one misses out, see you in class."

My point being is that any response from your website and the experience you create is a good response. It's when you get no response at all that you need to start worrying. But it doesn't stop there.

When a new prospect shows up to try your school, creating a great experience must still be top of your list. The experience they have includes how they are greeted when they arrive, the sign-up process, etc. Make your systems straightforward, professional, and smooth, day in and day out.

Always go back to the six human needs. Uncertainty is a huge one. We don't cope well in unfamiliar environments, especially ones that involve activities of being in close physical contact with others. Most students are jumping through so many psychological barriers to be at your school. Make sure everything you do helps them drop those barriers even more.

One of the best ways to create an experience for a new prospect is to be armed with information that shows you are interested in them as an individual, and that you have taken the time to find out more about them.

The simplest way to do this is to ask them to fill in a short, but useful survey when they opt-in for more information from your website, or book a class online. Send them to a web page that clearly shows you want to know more about the people who are coming to your school, by asking them three critical questions.

What is the pain they are trying to solve, the thing they would like to improve?

What would they like to gain by enrolling in your classes?

How much time are they willing to commit to achieve this?

Online surveys must be short, and I find that it's much easier to use multiple choice answers that broadly cover the main reasons why most people want to start training. You can then use this information in the first meeting to develop a more personal conversation.

For example: "Helen. I read that you're looking to learn practical self-defence to improve your confidence, so you feel safer when travelling home from work and can make better decisions if needed, and you're able to commit to eight training sessions a month, is that correct?"

Confirming you have read their information and would like to know more about them shows exceptional customer service. Whatever you are buying, be it a product or service, you always need to feel that it was made and designed for you. If you're going to invest your time and money in something, then there needs to be an emotional attachment. Otherwise, it will lose its value very quickly.

Using Helen as an example, although doing self defence training may make her feel safer, this of course is not the answer to be safer walking home from work, the way to feel safer is not to walk the route that makes her feel unsafe (we all know that) however, the mind does not work like this. The emotional brain is all powerful. Therefore you need to address the psychological need before offering a more logical option.

Helen "Yes, I often walk home later at night, and I think if I knew how to protect myself then I'd feel safer."

Me: "Absolutely. When training you will increase in confidence, and this will make you feel safer, and we'll also teach you how to make decisions a little faster by using more information that's around you, so you don't need to feel like you are unsafe, we'll teach you that you can avoid that feeling altogether."

Knowing more about the person allows you to begin the initial meeting warm with information, rather than going in cold. Knowing someone's name, the problems they are facing and what they would like to achieve goes a long way to show that you're serious, committed to your role and are focused on the needs of the new member.

The toughest part of the process of creating the experience is to get the new member (please remember I'm talking about the complete novice, not the person who's trained three other styles) to feel comfortable with engaging in the training and being the new person, especially if they are on their own.

We have a phrase that we use in our schools which is, "you're only the new member for one-night." It's essential to show people that the feeling of being new, different or an outsider is short term. Do all that you can to integrate them into the group, introduce them, get them training with one of your experienced members or assistant instructors who are patient and can ensure that they have a good time and feel part of the team straight away. We are pack animals. We survive in groups; there is nothing worse than feeling you are outside of a particular group, especially a new one. There must be a warm, welcoming approach.

There is a misconception that gaining experience is doing something there and then. It's not. Experience is what the training, lesson or information allows them to do afterwards. And the feeling it gives them. In other words, the experience is useless as you are gaining it, it only comes into play after the fact. Balance educational training with entertaining training. They must learn but also have fun. Ensure they enjoy themselves, that they gained something, engage with others and above all, feel part of the group. The fastest way that a child learns is through play. Playing is fun, and adults still love to play around. Make sure the lesson balances the freedom to try things, to learn and feel progress. If you're still running your school like the grandmaster walking around with an upside-down smile, continually hitting people with sticks (not literally I hope!) because they can't get it right the first time, then have it known that I'm praying for your failure. You are not helping the human race become better by teaching like this, neither are you growing your school as a happy place with a positive experience.

When building out your new student experience; set your personal expectations high. Do not settle for ok.

Walt Disney was obsessed with delivering magical experiences. He did so in a way that every one of his team members could follow. One of the hardest things is to get your team members to recreate the same experience that you can. Align your passions and your goals, so their burning desire pushes them as much as it does you. It will never be the same, but you can make damn sure you get it as close to it as possible.

CHAPTER CHECKPOINTS

Do you promote who you are or how you can help others?

Have you implemented a follow up system?

Are you clear on your ideal student/customer?

Chapter fourteen

The million dollar question.

"Not everything happens immediately. Things take time and patience is a skill."

Creating a fantastic experience for a new prospect is essential. It allows you to feel confident asking the million dollar question. "Would you like to join the school?"

Let's be crystal clear on something, asking this questions is a sales process, there is no getting away from it. Sales processes come in all shapes and sizes. Some ethical. Some not so much. Regardless of your opinion, you're attempting to sell something to somebody in the hope that they buy it.

The quicker you become ok with that, the better. I have met many school owners who say that they don't like to be too salesy. Get over it.

The more you think like that, the more frustrating growing a school will be.

There are various phrases like "selling is serving", or "selling without selling" or whatever play on words you want to use. It's merely about giving somebody a great experience from the beginning, adding value, and offering them the chance to continue having that experience over an extended period. One that helps them achieve their goals feel good and create new positives area within their life, all while making some fantastic new friends along the way.

Selling something to somebody does not have to be a hard approach, trying to force it down their throat, but at the same time, we must remember that we live in a very untrusting world. People these days struggle to make decisions about what they are going to have for dinner. So how hard do you imagine it is to commit to something new? Especially when their emotional brain is designed to keep them safe and limit change in their lives.

For someone to be sold to, they have to engage in the process of becoming a potential buyer; it's a two-way street. They may have initiated the process by showing up to your school, contacting you, or downloading some information that you made available.

How the sales process ends depends on whether the barriers, the things that stop the person committing to training, are overcome or not.

For the most part; we're intelligent creatures. We've kept ourselves alive while other species became extinct, so we know how to make our own decisions. They've just become more complicated as time went on. So as long as you have the right information, can process it, and are aware of the limiting barriers that may stop someone from joining, then everybody can choose.

Some people make all buying decisions based on emotions and then justify with logical reasons. That doesn't mean to say that you manipulate them to your advantage. If they align with your strengths then by all mean play on them.

Buying a new car is a fantastic example. Did you buy your last car because of its practicalities or, did you want that particular type of car? Think about that question based on when you bought it, not how you feel now.

I currently drive a top spec Ford Ranger. My reasons for having the Ford Ranger are practical (or so I tell myself), but if it were truly just for practical purposes, then I'd have bought the bottom of the range model, no sensors, no heated seats, no fancy gadgets…The purchase of the model was logical. All the fancy features? Emotional!

Previous to that I owned a brand new BMW. That was totally an emotional purchase. High spec, beautiful interior and way more than I needed. But once I owed it, and people starting asking me about the car. I began to make some rubbish up about the good monthly payment offers. That it was similar to other more practical cars that are available. That I was making long journeys and comfort was important. It's not true. I'm lying to myself and the other person. I just wanted to drive around in a BMW. It's as simple as that.

However, after a couple of months of driving, the BMW fantasy wore off a little, the service bills were high, I had to sell a kidney each time I changed a tyre. Regardless of this, instead of replacing the BMW for the Ranger, I very nearly bought the next BMW series. Why?

Once I had bought the car, BMW didn't just take my money and cut me off. I received various rewards. The monthly magazine came through the post, calls to see how I was getting on and much more. The most significant thing I received was the exceptional customer care when taking my car in for a service. Reminders of my appointment were sent, I had a personal service rep, excellent coffee in the waiting room and they cleaned my car after the service. They even sent me an iPhone video from the mechanic showing any work they recommended to be done. It was awe-inspiring. But was I paying for that type of service? Absolutely, I'd bought a BMW, but I was undoubtedly getting value for my money.

However, when I decided to buy the Ranger from Ford. That was another story. The sales process was a nightmare.

The sales rep could not decide on his own. He had to continually speak to Ron who was the all-knowing manager who sat in the back office like the Wizard of Oz. The sales rep would run back and forth asking Ron about my various requests. He couldn't close the deal alone or make me an offer to get me onboard. Eventually, when I ordered the vehicle, they contacted me and said I needed to pay more due to buying through a company (it's a commercial vehicle, of course, I'm going to buy it through a company, that's the whole point!), so I agreed to that. Then the date of delivery changed, and they told me it would be delivered on… wait for it… the 24th of December! Like that was going to happen.

It got to the point when I asked to speak to the all knowing Ron and said how unhappy I was with the service. How did Ron respond? "So do you want to cancel the order?"

I was shocked!

No offer to find out where the issues were, how he could help, and what they could do to save the sale of the £30,000 vehicle. No. He just offered me to cancel. My response was "Yes, cancel it".

Ron then refunded my deposit over the phone and before putting the phone down I said…"Ron, all I needed was some information, some communication to know what is happening. I'm trying to return my BMW at the same time as getting the Ranger. It's near the end of the year. I'm going away for Christmas. I've received multiple dates for the car to arrive and all during a time when I'm away. I've been offered no solution to help me arrange things, all I wanted was some options."

Ron went silent. He then realised that as a customer, I'd be left in the dark. The moment they had 'swiped' my credit card for the deposit, the deal was done. They were no longer interested, they didn't need to contact me, they'd tell me when to show up, and I'd have to be there, my commitments were not their concern. This would not have happened with BMW.

So you may ask, why did I continue to buy the Ranger? A simple logical reason. I was saving a massive amount off my VAT bill and my company tax bill. I'd had a very successful year, and my tax bills were big. Don't get me wrong. I'm all for paying tax, but if there are ethical ways to reduce the bills that I get some benefit, then common sense dictates I'm going to do that.

But you can see the apparent differences in adding value, offering service for a premium price, and delivering that personal service. It reduces frustration, creates loyalty, and a long-term membership to your brand.

This should be no different in your krav maga school, you need the same experience that BMW creates, ongoing, and therefore you should charge more if what you provide is high quality in both training and service.

When you go to ask the million dollar question, the new prospect should be clear on the enormous value they are getting in becoming a member of your school. Your price should reflect your value. Above all, you must deliver on that value every day; with no exceptions. And continue to do so long after the membership form is signed.

If you're providing value, you're doing everything to show the potential new member that when they join your school, it will be a fantastic experience and enhance their life.

But of course, they are going to have a variety of personal reasons that, even though they like the idea of joining, may prevent them from doing so.

We call these barriers to joining, and you must be aware of them. When the barriers appear, this is when you kick into second gear and have to show you understand their needs and their reservations. And that you'll do all you can to help them get over the barriers; providing that you genuinely believe that joining your school will have a positive impact.

Let's also be clear on something else. It's not right to try and sign up everyone to your school. Either your school doesn't meet their needs, they have a medical condition that may be worsened from the training, they may want to learn krav maga for unethical reasons, or it's clear they won't commit to the training and are doing it because it looked cool.

I have been to countless business development seminars, full of people who are either running businesses or want to build one. They are often self-employed or working in a small team. They are there for the buzz, to see the expert on stage talk about how they made five million in six seconds or got 200,000 subscribers using his secret strategy. The people are genuinely there to learn, are focused and feeling good. What they need is simple advice to implement. Instead, the experts on stage proceed to capitalise on the buzz in the room and use some NLP type sales tactics to get people to buy their latest business boot camp or online course, knowing full well that most of the people in the room do not need that right now. I'm all for offering products and services to people, but be clear on who it's for, and what it takes for somebody to implement what is being taught.

An excellent example of this is a public speaking course I once attended. It was a long course over five-days. I had always wanted to do the course, and I did find it incredibly useful. To be able to speak in public you have to be very clear on your content, your topic, and have some experience to share.

The majority of people on the course with me had no idea what they were going to speak about. One guy said to me he was in the property market and wanted to teach people how to buy and sell for profit. But he had no experience in this, but he was on a course to learn to speak about it to a room full of people, and he had no background in his chosen subject? That makes no sense.

There were also countless social media marketing consultants on the course with me, who were there because they wanted to learn how to speak about social media marketing, yet they had done very little actual social media marketing.

It turns out that many of these people on this public speaking course had been to one of these business conferences and got pulled in by the take my course and you'll be speaking to millions sales pitch, and they signed up. Although very nice people, with their heart in the right place, they didn't need a public speaking course. The £2500 they'd spent on it could have been put to better use studying their chosen industry more, and become an expert in their field by merely doing it more and growing the business.

The only reason I'm writing this book is that I have over ten years of experience growing adult krav maga schools, and I meet countless people who ask my advice. I've made some massive mistakes and had some considerable success, all from getting out there and doing it.

My point here is that even though someone shows up to your school thinking the training will be good for them, there will be a small percentage of those people who it's entirely wrong for. People like to follow the mass and don't want to feel excluded. They'll believe they need it when they don't.

In the few cases you have like this, be fair and honest with people about whether or not learning krav maga is right for them. Most people say that krav maga is for everyone; anyone can learn. I don't agree with that statement. There is much more than just the physical learning need to be considered.

Understanding what type of members you want in class, and searching for them, rather than taking anyone is essential. The moment you take this on as your strategy, then growing your school becomes more manageable and less frustrating. It may mean you take a longer road to your goals. However, nothing comes easy, or quickly, so settle in for the long journey.

Marketing genius Dan Kennedy says that if someone wants to buy a service, they know it's good for them, and they'd love to do it, only three barriers are stopping them.

Time: they cannot see how they can fit the activity into their already busy lives, they cannot make the most of what they are paying for and are not willing to change their priorities.

Money: they love the idea, but cannot afford it. Most people will use the excuse that it's 'too expensive'. There is a massive difference between something being expensive, and not being able to afford something.

Permission: often there is somebody else (usually a spouse) who has to agree that they can spend the money and the time doing this activity, it has to be a joint decision.

Let's look at each of those barriers in turn.

Barrier 1: Time

Time is the most precious thing that we have. It cannot be bought or taken back.

How we use that time is vital to everyone. We waste a tremendous amount of time, and therefore we believe we never have enough.

Have you also noticed that people use the words "spend my time"? Words are compelling, as they shape what you focus on and in turn how you behave. Smart people use the word invest their time.

You may now be thinking ok fair enough, it's just words but hang on a minute, which of the following phrases would convince you to take action?

"I've got a fantastic property deal, all you need to do is to spend £20,000, and you'll get a return on that for sure."

Or:

"I've got a fantastic property deal, all you need to do is invest £20,000, and you'll get a return on that for sure."

One of the definitions of the word invest is: "to use, give, or devote (time, talent, money etc.) to achieve something."

You must remember that when somebody is thinking about joining your school, one primary factor is what they are going to have to give up or change about their current schedule and structure. When someone decides not to join the school because 'they don't have enough time; I rarely accept that reason. It's usually because they don't deem taking a class as important to them.

Sometimes I may help them work out if that's the case. If they claim they "don't have enough time", then being honest, they are not the sort of person I'd want to join anyway. I know that the classes wouldn't be a priority. As a result, they'll progress slowly, get frustrated, and eventually quit. Sure, you could take their money for the short term, but it doesn't assist with long-term growth. Not only do you have to invest time in them while they are in your school, but you'll also waste precious resources chasing them when they don't turn up to lessons. Plus; I find it unethical taking someone's money knowing they won't be here in a month.

A classic example of this is a gentleman called Jeremy. He booked our trial class programme. After initially meeting one of the other instructors he had a lot of questions about joining, and the instructor felt it might be better if I was to speak with him, as I was due to be teaching at his next class.

When I met Jeremy, he started to explain that he was in the process of applying for custody for his young daughter and this was taking a lot of time and might take more in the future so only wanted to join for three months. Second, he said he already had some protective equipment, so didn't want to pay the joining fee. We give a free kit with the joining fee if you don't want it, that's ok, but it doesn't discount the cost, the price is the price.

Jeremy was also a very eccentric character, he couldn't concentrate for very long, and above all, struggled to follow instructions. I knew that he would be a challenge for any of our other members who would practise with him.

I made it clear to Jeremy that the price was set, that the joining fee and price was non-negotiable, and that our minimum commitment time was three months. You can't negotiate on something that's already discounted.

It was on the tip of my tongue to advise him not to join. However, in the back of my mind, I saw a guy who was in a custody battle for his daughter. It must have been quite stressful, and maybe he needed an outlet. Jeremy decided to join the school, and as you probably guessed, he was a complete nightmare.

He was always confirming when he could leave, and checking when his mandatory training period was up. He wanted to exchange other items of equipment from his joining pack as he already had some of it. He was always late for class, always forgetting his class sign-in card. The list goes on. And of course, a couple of months later he left, citing the custody battle as the reason.

I'm not heartless; I get that getting sole custody of your child is a big step, a big deal and needs focus. Which made me wonder why Jeremy would even consider starting krav maga when his life was already preoccupied with significantly essential things. I think it comes down to the fact that people don't like to be held back, they like to think they can do anything and everything whenever they want and to get quick results. The world doesn't work like that.

Success and progress are made through dedication and prioritising what is important right now in life. For Jeremy, that was the custody of his daughter, not starting a new activity that requires time and commitment. Had Jeremy had the ability to make that decision, he'd have probably saved us both a lot of time and him some money.

In my school, we do our best to avoid the Jeremy's and to advise them if the training is not right for them, but occasionally they slip through the net.

Joining the right people is a more pleasant experience, you'll build a membership base of like-minded individuals who share your values and are committed to progressing and learning what you can teach them. Take time to figure out your ideal member, and make sure you narrow your search to those types of people.

Barrier 2: Money

A common phrase I hear is that people do not have enough money, or want more money. But have you noticed that those people who say that cannot define precisely how much or why they need more?

Money can be an evil thing, but as they say, it makes the world go around. Money is something that changes hands. On a daily basis, there is plenty of it, the world never runs out, it's just some people give out more than they receive, some people earn more than they give out. Some people give out money that's not theirs; other people borrow money, give it out and then give it back and pay more for the privilege. Therefore a common barrier to joining your school is because "it's expensive". I don't agree with this argument unless you have found the same or a very similar service, with the same features and benefits for less money, then it can't be expensive.

It's expensive is an emotional response that I translate as follows.

"Krav maga training costs more than I'm willing to give of the money that I receive because if I do I will have a lot less or, will have nothing or, will have to sacrifice something else." Let's get real. Before thinking about starting krav maga training with a professional club (in the UK), you could take a wild guess that it's going to be between £50 - £80 per month depending on where you live, and what the school offers, so if you know you do not have that disposable income, then why would you show up?

That's no different to me turning up to the Ferrari showroom, knowing that it's going to cost me at least over six figures to buy one, and then when the salesperson tells me the price, I say "Oh, that's expensive, that's more than I thought."

This is utterly emotional behaviour; there is no logic here.

There is also no such thing as a free lunch. If you say to someone, your training is £50 a month, and they say "that's expensive"… if you then said £49 would that be expensive or acceptable? This then brings on the whole subject of psychological pricing. That's a big subject to talk about, and I recommend you check out Nick Kolenda's work if you want to find out more and structuring your pricing for value and perception.

My point being is that when money genuinely is the barrier, you have to either establish if the individual really can afford it. In which case you shouldn't try to sell them a membership. Or, is it the fact that they have to make a change in their spending habits to join? For some people, making sacrifices are too hard which suggests your school is not the best fit.

You must be clear on explaining the cost of joining your school, show the value they are getting and how that breaks down. For example, our current offer is: £79 a month for eight classes per month, so that's £9.87 per class. If you want to attend more than eight sessions, it's free. We don't ask you for more if you're willing to invest more time to get better, we want to help you do that. When people see that they can get more than what they are paying for, it adds enormous value

If someone appears to think that "it's expensive" I often wondered what they would expect to pay? If it was £69 a month? Would that make a difference? Is £2.50 a week critical to that person? If my life is dependent on whether I have that £10 or not each month, I've got more important priorities than joining a krav maga school.

Most of the time it's purely emotional. The question is, how do they perceive £79 compare to what they are getting, and how does that translate to the goals they are trying to reach?

When potential new members have challenged the price, I press them: "what price did you expect it to be?" To which I get answers like "the karate club down the road is £6 per class." But we don't teach karate. It's not the same thing. This, through no fault of your customers own, is a lack of education about what your classes are about. One that is your responsibility to give.

If someone suggests they thought it would be £60 a month rather than £79 a month, then I say I'd not feel comfortable joining them knowing that £15 is critical to their monthly living, as I think that was unfair on them. We all know that £15 is what many people would spend on the first round of drinks in the bar, or on multiple TV upgrade packages… sometimes people need to be clear on whether they want to invest their hard-earned cash in krav maga training, or whether it just sounded cool.

Barrier three: Permission

If you've been teaching krav maga for a while and met a lot of potential new students, you'll have no doubt heard the phrase "1 need to speak to my partner/wife/husband."

This is an entirely valid reason not to join immediately, and they have to give it some thought.

Relationships and marriage are partnerships, long-term agreements to share things in life, and time is one of them. Getting the ok to spend time away from family is the right thing to do. How people go about that's a different matter (usually completely the wrong way!) Nevertheless, it's a factor and one that you must appreciate.

Let the person go and speak to their partner, and then follow them up later and see what you can make work. If their relationship is good, there will be some flexibility for personal activities, and it's likely they will join.

Since reading the books by Dan Kennedy and understanding that pretty much, all these barriers, time, money, and permission are the general reasons why someone will not join my school, life has become much easier for me. In fact, I'm sincere and upfront with the new student about the fact if they decide not to join, it's because of one of these reasons. I don't dress it up at all.

If your school is professional, the training is progressive, safe, welcoming, they had a good time, and it would help them achieve their goals, then there is no need for you to continue to go on about how amazing it is. They get it, they understand it. It's not whether they liked it or not I mean, we may all have dragged ourselves to the gym, but we never have a terrible workout, right? Krav maga is fun, it's cool, and you do learn some great stuff with awesome people, and of course, it may save your life one day.

Make sure you are clear with the common barriers, how to spot them, and how when you should overcome them, or part ways with a potential new student until it is a better fit.

The sales process in our school is straightforward now. I have moved away from complex sales processes. We use an iPad presentation that shows what they get, what it costs and then we answer some frequently asked questions.

I'm very upfront about everything. We talk personally to the new student to outline their needs and commitment. If it's right for them, they will join. If they need to get over one of the barriers, let them go and think that through but follow them up, do not force the sale by continually discounting and giving more away.

Of course, you must have a joining offer. Everyone loves free stuff and paying later, but it doesn't mean you continually move the goal posts to get them to sign-up. That sort of student will not stay in your school, which presents a retention problem and as we all know, losing students feels personal. The constant battle to balance new members joining with current leaving members is a never-ending story.

You cannot solve the puzzle of how to sign up and keep everyone, but you can maintain it at a reasonable level. This makes long-term planning much more manageable. When growth is steady, you can forecast your finances, and live more peacefully day to day, enjoying what you do.

If someone does not join on the night of their first class, it doesn't mean all is not lost, far from it, they might just be getting over a barrier and not mentioned it to you.

Have you ever looked at a product or service online, and then suddenly started seeing adverts for that product or service on your computer screen all the time, as you visit different websites, or scroll on social media?

As many of you will know, this is called a re-targeting pixel.

The moment you look at that product or service, the company puts a code in your computers history and then with some smart technology, it can keep showing it to you wherever you've been searching on the internet.

This is a fundamental explanation of how it works, but I use it to illustrate something.

People rarely buy the first time they see something or try something, unless they are immediately emotionally attached to it or, the sales process was very compelling, and they needed to get that product or start that service straight away. Most people need seven or eight exposures to a business before they even consider making a purchase. So if a student does not sign-up to your school the first time, all is not lost. You are just at the beginning of your sales cycle.

A colleague of mine told me recently about when he'd gone to help another school owner on the launch day of his new krav maga school.

The new school owner had managed to get 40 new potential students to the launch day and proceeded to teach an excellent first class. At the end of the class, he gave a compelling offer for people to join, of which 1 out of the 40 took up the offer and joined. The remainder did not.

My colleague then asked the school owner what the was going to do with the other 39 people, to which he answered: "They don't want to do it, let them leave."

I was shocked when he told me this.

Maybe they were not ready to commit right now, but with some follow-up phone calls, invites to future classes to find out more about them, to discuss the barriers they need to cross, I guarantee, will have seen more students joining the school further down the line.

Get in touch with them, find out what they are looking to achieve, why they came in the first place, and what is stopping them from committing. You must do this until they tell you, categorically, that it's not for them.

Until someone tells me NO, then they are still interested… simple!

Please do not read this as pushy sales processes. It's not. But the fact is that life is busy, people have so much going on day to day with work and family pressures, often finding time to do something for themselves is hard, and they will only make excuses not to do it.

Sometimes they need someone to talk it through with, and to be sure that you, their potential instructor, have their best interests at heart. Which you must have. Take the extra time. The best relationships are built on getting to know people first and are often long-term relationships with loyalty, focus, dedication, and some great experiences along the way.

Treat every new potential student as an individual, and keep doing that when they become members. You never know, they might become an instructor one day, helping you grow your school.

You don't know who you don't know so it's exciting where your new relationships might take you. My best instructors are those who started out as students with me. Some rock stars have even gone on to work with me running their own schools. For that, I am immensely proud. Considering they've been going strong for over a decade now I'd like to think I've done some things right. Otherwise, it's unlikely people would stay.

CHAPTER CHECKPOINTS

What is your sales process?

Are you clear on the three barriers (time/permission/money)?

Are you offering a BMW style service?

Chapter fifteen

Did you order the code red?

"Learn to love the numbers"

If the title of this chapter means nothing to you, then you're younger than me, and I'm insanely jealous! The title comes from an iconic part of the film 'A Few Good Men' starring Tom Cruise and Jack Nicholson. It's a legal drama about a Navy commander, where Tom Cruise (a Navy lawyer called Daniel Kaffee) has to prove that Jack Nicholson (a Navy commander called Colonel Jessop) ordered the illegal code red punishment of a recruit called Santiago that resulted in his accidental death.

If you have not seen the film, I'm about to spoil it for you.

At the end of the film, Tom Cruise is cross-examining Jack Nicholson in the courtroom and is doing his best to get Jack to admit he ordered the code red. Jack does everything to bypass the question, but when the frustration gets too much, he admits it under pressure. He tells the truth…

Here is an excerpt from the film:

Jessep (Nicholson): You want answers?

Kaffee (Cruise): I think I'm entitled to them.

Jessep: You want answers?

Kaffee: I want the truth!

Jessep: You can't handle the truth! Son, we live in a world that has walls. And those walls have to be guarded by men with guns. Who's going to do it? You? I have a greater responsibility than you can fathom. You weep for Santiago, and you curse the marines. You have that luxury. You have the luxury of not knowing what I know: that Santiago's death, while tragic, probably saved lives. And my existence, while grotesque and incomprehensible to you, saves lives...You don't want the truth. Because deep down, in places you don't talk about at parties, you want me on that wall. You need me on that wall.

We use words like honour, code, loyalty...we use these words as the backbone to a life spent defending something. You use them as a punchline. I have neither the time nor the inclination to explain myself to a man who rises and sleeps under the blanket of the very freedom I provide, then questions the manner in which I provide it! I'd rather you just said thank you and went on your way. Otherwise, I suggest you pick up a weapon and stand a post. Either way, I don't give a damn what you think you're entitled to!

Kaffee: Did you order the code red?

Jessep: (quietly) I did the job you sent me to do.

Kaffee: Did you order the code red?

Jessep: You're goddamn right I did!!

As you can see, he does all he can to avoid the direct answer, he knows it will get him in trouble but pride takes over, and under pressure, he answers with the truth, then realises that he's now in a lot of trouble. His status and position came before the truth and saying and doing what was right.

When people ask my advice about growing their school, I asked them, in my own way, if they ordered the code red, and the conversation that happens after this question almost always sounds a lot like that courtroom...

It goes something like this:

Me: Do you know the financial state of your school?

Them: I've got 50 adults members, 125 junior members.

Me: Do you know the financial state of your school?

Them: I've money in the bank, we're not in debt, we pay the bills.

Me: Do you know the financial state of your school?

Them: I've been running the school for years, we've always joined new members every year, we lose some but that's the same as all schools, our training is the best in the area. Etc.

Me: Do you know the financial state of your school?

Them: What do you mean? Of course, I do.

Me: What was your income last month and your net profit?

Them: You want the truth?

Me: If you want me to help you, then that would be nice!

Them: I have no idea about the financial state of my school!!

Knowing the actual month by month accounting figures of your school provides you with accurate information that does not lie. By calculating your numbers, you can highlight strengths and gaps in your organisation.

Do not mistake this for "are you making lots of money?" That would only be the case if making money was your goal. However, for a business to run and turn a profit, you need to map out your incomings and outgoings month in and month out. This includes wages, rent, bills and your salary, and other overheads. What did you plan to have versus what have you got? Do those numbers match?

It's no different to any other target, such as training to lose weight. What weight did you want to be? What weight are you at this point? If both of those figures are the same, then great, things are moving forward. If you lost more weight than you planned, you're exceeding the goal. But if you're underachieving, then changes need to be made, or you need to work out why it's not going to plan.

I've met countless school owners who think "bills just come out of nowhere". This isn't the case. You didn't focus on the finances and were too lost in everything else. Finances run precisely the same way as trying to get fit. If you do not have a plan and track the results, you will merely run month by month, biting your fingernails because if a sudden change arises, you know things will be hard.

I've already spoken about uncertainty and how we don't deal with it well, and one of the more significant fears is the fear of loss or not having enough to live. When I say enough, that does need to be defined. When somebody says "I want to earn just enough to [insert life reason]." That doesn't wash with me. You need to specify a number. If you don't, how can you track it? What is enough? It makes no sense. Or when I hear "I want enough to be comfortable". Comfortable is a feeling, not a number, and emotions go up and down depending on your mood, your environment and whatever is happening in your life at the time.

I was having a conversation with my coach Ray recently who said that most businesses operate for one year, and then repeat that first year, ten times. Rarely do they grow, adapt, and change. What they did for that first year worked, so they kept on doing it. The problem with having the same results in year ten that you did in year one will be quite demoralising and then you'll fall into that trap of saying things like "I've worked hard all my life and got nothing to show for it, times are hard, it's tough to make a living." They are excuses. It just means you didn't take the results from year one and work out a plan to improve them incrementally over the next few years.

It's said that 50% of businesses fail within the first five years. I believe the reason for that is a lack of reviewing past results and adapting accordingly. Instead, people rest on the relative success of the previous year and hope that the next year will be the same, or maybe better yet without any formal plan how to make it better. Which then becomes about asking the same questions about how to improve year in and year out, yet never implementing them. Hope is not a strategy. That type of emotional roller coaster is ok to ride when you are younger but trust me, as you get older, it will get tiresome and stressful.

If you have no clue about how your school performed financially last year with accurate, professionally prepared accounts, then you have no way of knowing where you need to make changes to grow and enjoy the fruits of your labour.

Things take time. This is not something I'd expect you to do in the first year, or maybe even the second but by year three, you had better start getting to grips with it. Here is how I think things play out, from my own experience.

Year 1: Your school is set-up. There is some investment, the whole set up process is fun, exciting and challenging, there are no real expectations except to get going and get the fundamentals in place.

Year 2: Your school is established. You start to enjoy it more, maybe going on some courses, recruiting an instructor from your student base, running some more events, pro-shop products and pushing more money into nice shiny things that make you feel good, the money is flowing, and life feels good.

Year 3: Your school continues to grow, more staff is required, you might move premises, the website needs updating, you may hit VAT levels, you may decide to become a limited company as its more tax efficient than working as a self-employed individual. You may restructure the school based on the elaborate advice from a tax accountant who specialises in martial arts training. All in all, it's less fun. Growth is a fantastic thing, but it creates more plates to spin.

It's at this time when you need to focus your energy on getting much clearer on the financial state of your school on a regular basis. Ideally monthly. Within ten days of the end of the month, you must know how your school performed last month. Is this hard? Absolutely. Are you going to need help to achieve it? Damn right you are. But it's the most valuable thing you could invest in for your long-term future.

Another useful phrase that was said to me once was: "Most people let their accountant tell them how much tax they owe at the end of the year. I prefer to tell the accountant how much I owe." That advice hit me like a straight punch to the head, and I set myself on a path to be able to do just that.

If an accountant says to you "Well done you made £10,000 profit last year", two things are likely to be sure:

You have no idea if that's good or not, you will emotionally decide whether £10,000 is a lot of money to you, versus the time and effort you put in.

You probably wonder why you do not have that £10,000 in the bank right now.

Every year I set out to make sure that those two things are utterly irrelevant to me. If I profit £25,000, I will either know that's good, because my target was £15,000 or, it was terrible because my aim was £35,000.

If it was good, why was it good? Where did we make more? What did we spend less on? What made us £10,000 richer? Because whatever it was, I'll make sure we do more of it.

If the answer was no, then I want to work out where we didn't make the money we planned, or where we spent more than we should have, then I can do something about that.

I fully understand that the currents state of my bank account will always be different to the accounting figures that I receive. One is a record of the recent past. The other is what's happening right now.

When you genuinely get to know your financials, it can be a huge shock, just because money flows through your accounts and you get paid each month doesn't mean you own a profitable school. Far from it. And let's not make the mistake of thinking that lots of students implies the business is turning a profit. I have met schools with 100's of students who are barely making any profit because their pricing model is completely wrong compared to the way the school is set-up.

Getting a good bookkeeper and accountant is one of the keys to financial success plus making a clear statement about what income you would like to make, what salary you will take, and what profit will be left at the end. A clear statement does not involve the word 'enough' it involves exact numbers, which are achievable based on your current structure.

When I was working at the first school I set-up, I will never forget a meeting with the accountant that had one day. We were set up as a limited company, he presented the accounts to us and said: "You guys did well. You made a £60,000 net profit." You may think that I was happy about that, but the truth is that I didn't know what it meant. Seriously, I had no idea what net profit was, or what it meant. I cannot remember what I replied.

Whether being naive in this circumstance was good or not I'm unsure. Being naive meant that greed did not set in, but at the same time, we did no analysis on why we had made that sort of money.

Being clear on your numbers can often save you from sleepless nights, and having to 'find money' when you need it. If I'm honest with you, it's still something that messes with my mind a little. My brand has not been set-up with the ultimate intention of making a fortune, instead our focus was and always has been providing quality instruction, dedicating the time to helping others is the main purpose. Of course, it's still a business, and it still needs to profit. Some years I will be happy with the performance, other years I will be disappointed. My accountant can sit in front of me and say 'well done, you pretty much hit targets this year', and even though I understand about targets and budgeting, and even though I've just written this chapter about being clear, emotion still takes over. I expect too much sometimes.

Money can mess people up. It really must be seen as a tool. I will never forget the conversation I had with a city banker, who told me he had bought a Porsche, but then a few months later he wanted a Lamborghini. He contacted the dealership and two days before going to buy the new car, he cancelled the appointment and went and bought a Ford Focus. Why? He said that process never ends, short-term material gains wear out, getting a bigger house or a faster car are all very nice things, but they are by no means a measure of happiness. My experience with the billionaire showed me that.

What does provide happiness is knowing where you are at on a day to day basis. That you are on the right path to the goal you set or, that you are slightly off track. It's time to get to work and make changes to steady the course. This is all part of the fun of running a school, enjoying the journey, the learning and getting results, with results you can do things, you can adapt, educate and improve. Without results, you can merely hope.

As a business grows, inevitable tax bills will increase. Personal tax, VAT, (and if you are an Ltd company) corporation or company tax as it's known in some countries. Having worked with my business coach Ray, he would always use a phrase "I love paying more tax." I used to look at him as if to say he was mad. "I love paying more tax, as it means I made more money." This is a very true statement and one I have had to learn to agree with. That's until it's time to pay the VAT bill of course!

VAT is something that you don't mess with. As my friend James says, VAT is not your money. It's the government's money that you're collecting for them.

If your club is growing and you are VAT registered, take heed of that advice and use it as a discipline to always pay your VAT on time. Otherwise, in effect, you spent someone else's money, and that's ethically wrong.

Getting a good accountant who understands your business is the first step to knowing your numbers. They must show an interest in what you do, and suggest the right structure for your business, and what would be best to help you achieve your goals. An accountant will show less interest if they ask you what your plan is, and you can't answer. The professional ones will be ok with that answers for a couple of years, but in year three if you're still moaning and growing about tax bills and the state of your business, they will lose interest, as they will know you have no plan.

The question is, where are you right now in the growth of your school? If you're self-employed, and it's just you working in the school, then you're at the starting point. You effectively own a job right now, and your goal is to be financially stable enough to get some help, another instructor or some admin assistance as you move to become a company.

If you have some instructors helping you, and some admin or sales staff, then the next step is to make sure that everyone has defined roles, and the structure is solid so you can grow, enjoy it and have some free time for yourself. Allowing you to spend your day doing the things you want to do.

My instructor Eyal Yanilov is (at the time of writing) 58 years old and still travels the world sharing his knowledge. I'm not sure I will do it to his level of commitment, he is a crusader after all, but certainly to be still sharing what I have learnt, helping others to achieve their goals will always be a part of what I do.

How much money will I be making then? How many staff will I have? Who will be running the business? Without getting clear on my numbers, month in month out, I may end up doing it as a necessity at 65 rather than through choice, and that's by far less appealing.

If we ever met, and I ask you if you know your numbers, a confident and straightforward YES, will be the most impressive thing that someone can ever say to me when discussing their business. I don't care how beautiful your training centre is, how many students you have or the website changes you're making. I want to know if it's tracked, planned and all part of the long game because if it's, that's a conversation I'd love to continue… as I will likely be learning from you.

If you know your numbers, you can set target and goals. Then you can begin to focus on the best way to attract and keep the right members as long as possible. Then you can start to understand what is working and what is not so you can make changes.

Once you learn to adapt, you can grow your school to a point where your team and systems run harmoniously. With accurate measures in place to track your progress. These methods leave creative room for new ideas to flourish. Helping you discover ways to keep your members as long as possible. After all, that's how you'll turn a profit.

CHAPTER CHECKPOINTS

Do you know your numbers?

Do you know your NUMBERS?

DO YOU KNOW YOUR NUMBERS?

Chapter sixteen

The price is right.

"Your time is valuable. Charge the right price."

If you know your numbers, you can then make smart, informed decisions about whether or not your prices are right. Accurate pricing is something that many school owners struggle with. Whether it's down to the fear of loss or failure. Most of the time, the school owners I've met are drastically undercharging for the value they can give to people's lives.

The first book I read by one of my training mentors, Sgt. Rory Miller was Meditations on Violence It was a booked that changed everything about the way I think about teaching self-defence.

After finishing the book, I remember thinking that I really want to meet Rory and attend one of his seminars or courses.

I saw a Facebook post that said Rory was teaching his Scenario Training Instructor Programme in the UK. Here it was, a chance to meet the person who wrote the book that influenced me.

I read the Facebook post and clicked through to the website to read the information, and the smile slowly dropped from my face. I was having second thoughts as to whether I should attend Rory's course, I didn't think it would be worth it and might be a waste of time. Why? I saw the price; it was so cheap!

Here was a guy who had a massive influence on my abilities as an instructor, and he was charging £125 for a three-day course. My initial thoughts were that this course might not actually be that good as Rory was selling his valuable information cheaply. I didn't know at the time the prices were only so low because he'd underpriced his service, and didn't have a lot of experience in this area of business.

Price perception is something you need to be acutely aware of. It's also something that people make decisions on, before and after they join your school. This is why I do not advertise our prices on our website. People make snap judgements on money, without understanding what they get for it.

I expected that Rory would be charging at least three times as much for that course, and to be honest; I'd have paid over £1000 to be trained by Rory, as his book had influenced me so much. I'm happy to say that since meeting him and becoming friends, he took my advice and raised his prices to what he deserves to charge based on his experience.

Setting prices can be scary for school owners. At the same time, one of the most significant stresses is not making enough money. Let's talk about setting up your prices for the first time.

I always like to think about things on a per class basis. What is one person paying for my time for one class? What fee am I willing to work for, and what reflects the value we offer? In addition to that, what are my costs? How much does it cost me to run the school?

All of this need to be taken into consideration.

Also, are you offering a premium service? Are you providing the best training and assistance in your area? Do you give it 100% when it comes to customer service, support, and offering massive value?

The term massive value is used a lot, but it's rarely explained. By definition, it means that what people receive for the price they pay seems equal to, or more than what they are paying.

Going back to my BMW story, they offered this to me in every area, and I paid the price for that. You must do the same. There are various models of BMW available with additional features that can be added or taken away. Krav maga training is different. The training is what it is; you either do more of it or less. There are no other variations.

Many school owners used the 'three-tier pricing structure, for example…

Four lessons per month = £45.

Eight lessons per month = £55.

Twelve lessons per month = £65.

I'm not a big fan of this pricing structure. I'm not saying it doesn't work. I understand that there have been many studies that say people will choose the middle option with three-tier pricing.

However, I believe in charging for your time, not how much they want to attend. It's not like with BMW where different options give you better value. With krav maga, you cannot change the service. You're merely quoting a price on how much they use it. It's not as if you're going to reduce the quality of your teaching if they pay less or not teach specific techniques; that would be unethical.

Whether they attend four or fourteen classes a month, you're giving 100% dedication to making them better. They are paying to come for the information you're sharing, not for the time they spend there. They are paying for the education, the time frame of the class is based on how much information people can retain, and also how much they can sustain physically. For most of your students, this will only be an hour.

If somebody wants to practice more, why should they be punished for wanting to get better and improve? If you're going to make more money from people wanting to train more or focus on a particular area, then offer private lessons or workshops for more extended periods of training. This unlocks a different level of service and should be charged accordingly.

The other reason I avoid a three-tier pricing system is cash flow. It's quite hard to forecast your potential sign-ups as you have no idea how many people will sign up and for which tier. That's why I prefer one price, but make sure that the value is evident in that one price, make it simple, all-inclusive and hugely valuable to the new student.

I use our pricing model for many reasons. On average, attending a training class eight times per month is achievable for most people, plus we believe if you train less than this, your progression will be slow and frustrating, and you'll probably leave, as you won't see the results. I've never understood the attitude of people who want to do an activity that's physical but do it once a week. Your body does not adapt to the training and be more of a hindrance than a help.

The more decisions people have to make, the harder it is. When we tell new students that they are paying for their eight times a month, but if they want to train more they can, at no further charge. They like it. They love the flexibility. They also don't have to count their sessions. When we tried and tested the three-tier pricing model, I've had many students get in touch and say that they want to train more so can they pay £10 extra that month. This is an administrative nightmare. I merely wish to charge the money monthly and focus on delivering great training. Not have to worry about processing and extra £10 every couple of days.

I'm in the business of making people a better version of themselves. If I don't see them very much, I can't help them. If someone wants to pay £30 a month and train once a week, I know that I will struggle to help them make progress. Also, it will frustrate me as much as it will them. I'm not happy about that.

The other way to ensure you're charging the right price for what you provide is to offer more value off the mats. Each year I work on something that will add more value to the memberships of our schools, here's what we do at the moment:

We have private Facebook groups where we post content and training videos from various classes.

We publish a full-colour 26-page magazine every eight weeks full of useful training information and articles from multiple people.

I send a weekly email out to all our members with some training ideas, a story or something of interest. I do this without fail. Every week. Remember, consistency is critical.

We have an online members platform which offers training videos, grading guidance, health and fitness advice, digital copies of the magazine and much more.

We offer free accelerator workshops four times a year where they can attend for four hours, and we'll focus on a specific topic.

Think about this; I don't want 100 students all paying me different prices for different things for six months, I want 100 students paying a set amount (that may rise a little over time) for six years. That way I can focus on their training and development, and not worry if we have enough money to pay the bills.

Is it hard work? Of course. But what did you expect? That charging the right price and keeping your members while joining more was going to be easy? Get your head in the game of focus, hard work, and progress. The same way you do with your own personal krav maga training.

The same goes for your joining fees. Most schools charge a joining fee. It's expected in the martial arts and fitness world. There is an administrative fee to join the school. Somebody has to spend time setting up the membership, communicating with the new student, and making sure they are set up, there is a fee associated with that. But, the customer can't see that hard work, so we need to offer more value.

Much like rock climbing or horse riding, there is essential equipment that's needed for krav maga training for safety, and of course to make sure your brand looks premium and professional. If you join a krav maga school, you pay your joining fee, and then you are told you need to go and hunt on the internet to buy your training equipment and also pay for your uniform. Instead, we take the hassle out of joining the school and get the new member on the training mats as soon as you can by supplying them with the equipment that they need to get started.

Our joining fee at present is £147 and includes all of the equipment and uniform that the new members need to get started in training.

"Ah but John, you're charging for the equipment and uniform, not the joining fee. You are just playing a sales game." I disagree. If somebody turns up and has all the protective equipment they need, they still pay. The uniform and equipment is a gift. Yes, we absorb the cost but that's our loss, and our choice and if you know your numbers, you know it makes sense. We want that new member on the mats and progressing as soon as possible. Besides, we want everyone in the same uniform. It looks professional from a window shopping perspective, both on and offline.

Accurate pricing also includes raising your prices. I know school owners who have not increased their rates in over eight years. This is just crazy. The costs to run your business have changed over the last eight years. Therefore you must raise your prices.

But there is a reason that school owners do not raise prices. Yes, you've guessed it, our old friend FEAR is back again. Fear that people will leave, or that others will judge why they are raising prices. Let me tell you now that people expect prices to increase. It doesn't mean they have to like it, remember, we don't like change. So your job is to clearly explain the price increase, add some value to it, and soften the blow as much as you can.

If people quit due to a £5 or £10 raise in prices, then it's likely they are going to stop anyway, and they will use the fee increase as their reason to leave. Again, if that £10 is critical as to whether they live comfortably, or are struggling, I'd rather they invest the £79 in something else to make their life a little easier. I'll sleep better knowing that.

Before raising prices, make sure you map out what value you are going to deliver, and then take some educated guesses as to who might use the price increase as a reason to leave. These are usually the people who don't train much and show little commitment.

We recently raised the prices in our school and launched our online members' platform as part of it. One member, (who we thought might leave anyway) used the price increase to say it was now 'too expensive' as she didn't have the disposable income and needed to cut back.

Three days after leaving, she is posting on Facebook about the music concert she is going to, after just spending £80 on each ticket. You see my point. People struggle to be honest and will do all they can to stop themselves from feeling like they are quitting, or giving up.

Be clear on your pricing, do not undercharge, and do not overcharge, be able to explain your price breakdown and the value they are getting, and you will join the right people. Set out a plan to raise your prices over specific time frames, add more value to what your members are getting already, and I guarantee you that everything will be fine as long as you communicate it in the right way. People expect to pay a higher price for higher value. They do it every day when buying other products and services. Your school is no different.

Something else I also believe in (for adults) is paid for introduction classes. We do not offer free lessons for adults. Instead, we provide a low priced option to come and experience krav maga over a period of three classes, plus they get access to a getting started video that helps them begin learning from the moment they book their first class. Remember, first impressions count.

There are many thoughts on paid introduction classes versus free ones. My experience is that charging for your time tends to attract the more serious people. You might meet less of them, but they are decent people. If someone is going to invest a small amount of money, let's say £19.99 to come and give krav maga a go, then I can be sure they are relatively serious.

During the short-term, we offered free intro classes. The world's population of idiots seemed to be turning up to learn. They were not serious. Sometimes showing up but often not. As they had not invested anything in the experience, they had no vested allegiance in being there.

As we said before, tracking your results between ideas is essential. By all means, test the free intro offer with a paid for a trial class programme and see what works. I assure you one will be a lot more work than the other, and they will deliver very different results. It's good practise to take the best results and run with them. Your goal is to meet the right people, and that means being a little selective from the very beginning.

CHAPTER CHECKPOINTS

What do you charge and why?

How often do you raise your prices?

Does your price mirror your value?

Chapter seventeen

The blacklist.

"Create consistent ways to keep people motivated"

If you think about it, running a school is actually pretty simple. You only have two primary goals:

Attract the right new students

Keep as many of your existing students as you can.

How you do that?

Be clear about your why.

Create a team of rockstars to help you.

Focus on creating a fantastic experience for your students.

Invest in coaching or mentorship.

Be mindful where and with whom you invest your money.

Create an online presence.

Choose the marketing methods that work for you based on proven results.

Get your price right.

Providing exceptional training, balance entertainment with education.

Know your numbers.

Growth is exciting, but it's not always consistent. When it comes to growing your school, you'll discover moments we call flat points. These are times where you feel stagnant; your business does not seem to be moving, and you are and not hitting your targets.

When you reach these points, there is a simple solution. Highlight where your problem areas are and focus your efforts there, adjusting accordingly. These moments can be frustrating, challenging, and feel like you're running the wrong way up an escalator. One student joins two leave. It appears to be never-ending.

The most challenging plateau I have found with adult members is the growth from 145 students to 200. Now, you could argue that 145 members in a school all paying premium pricing is a pretty good school. If that is your target, that's excellent. My goal wasn't to grow to 145 and stop. I wanted to keep pressing forwards.

In business, we cannot control everything. We can, however, take reasonable steps to limit fallout by being very clear on our financial numbers from the offset. After all, how can we grow if we aren't striving towards a goal? Consider this in mountaineering. Would you continue to climb the mountain not knowing where the summit was? In the hope, it was around the next corner? That's why being clear on what you want and why you want it is critical to your success.

For example, what does 150 adult members all paying £70-100 a month mean to you and your family? Is it that the only goal or does it feed into a more significant purpose? If your goal helps you achieve what you want; congratulations. You're on the right path. If it doesn't, you need to think bigger.

Your financial targets represent people who pay you for what you give to them. But at the end of the day, they will likely stop paying you if they feel they are no longer getting value, their goals are not being met, and most importantly, that you do not care about them individually.

You need to keep a happy balance between signing new members and retaining the students that you have. Common sense says that retention costs you less in both time and money.

Why do schools lose members and struggle to keep them in training?

I believe it's all to do with what we feel and perceive is right, versus the harsh truth. There is something less emotional about keeping members compared to signing a new one. Signing a new one feels like a win. But keeping new members and doing what you need to so that we ensure they are getting value from what they are paying for and staying with you longer doesn't seem so fulfilling, and it becomes one of those tasks that becomes tactically avoided, you get complacent and ended up panicking, or getting upset when they leave.

If I ask most school owners to tell me the one thing they need to do more of, it will always be reducing student attrition.

People will always avoid the things they dislike and instead focus on the tasks they enjoy. This is human nature, I do it, and you will do it. But you have to fight this.

Sometimes we have to do things out of necessity. As ex-Navy Seal, leadership coach and MMA gym owner Jocko Willink says: "discipline equals freedom." I couldn't agree more. You have to fight through the pain of doing things you don't like.

For example, writing this book is arduous. It's tough staying motivated to get up early to put pen to paper while the world sleeps. I do it anyway. My long-term gain is more significant than my short-term pain, and so it drives me to push forward.

The effort you need to make to retain your students is minimal. You need to get into the habit of repeating these seemingly insignificant small actions of showing you care but over time:

Making follow up calls.

Checking that people are hitting their goals.

Monitoring people's grading progressions.

Reviewing that people are ok when they do not show up in class.

Celebrating personal achievements with them.

These actions make a huge impact. As you don't see an instant win, it's easy not to appreciate their value.

When you have a handful of students, this is effortless to maintain. When you have a full-time business, you need a system to follow so that you can stay true to your goal. You need a way to monitor the results each month and the number of students training, compared to those paying. I call this the blacklist.

Most people don't like the term. Probably because of the association with the TV show, or the fact it often means that people on the list are bad and have done something wrong.

On the contrary. I call my system the blacklist because it pushes me to take action. Seeing a visibly long blacklist makes me want to limit the number of people on it. Not being on the list means that the student is, as far as I can reasonably assume, happy and is getting value from the school as they are using the services, attending classes, and progressing. If they aren't, it means I need to improve something to help them have a better experience.

We usually add people to the list if they haven't been to class in over three weeks. We keep track of absenteeism because it's essential for us to make sure they are ok. Plus they are paying for a service, and we want to make sure they are getting what they pay for. If they aren't attending, is it something about the school keeping them away? How can we improve upon that?

I have met many school owners who complain that they lose so many students but convince themselves that there is nothing they can do about it. To a point, I'd agree. There is a percentage of skipped classes that you can't help. For others, it's probably just a case of life getting in the way. You've been through it yourself, things mount up and become overwhelming. Suddenly, your ability to prioritise what you want to do over what you need to do becomes disproportioned, and you fall behind. Your students are the same. The more time that passes. The harder it is to return to class. A nudge from you might be the push they need to get back into the routine.

There is a book called Never Split the Difference by Chris Voss (which I think helps here.) Chris is a former hostage negotiator with the FBI. He discusses three categories of information that negotiations fall into:

Known, knowns.

Known, unknowns.

Unknown, unknowns.

A known, known is something that we know that we know. For example, we know that Ben Jones has not been training for two weeks and we know that's because he's on holiday.

A known, unknown is something that's possible yet has not been confirmed. For example, we know that Ben Jones said he was going on holiday at some point but are not sure if it's right now.

An unknown, unknown is something that we don't know and would not even consider or had knowledge of. For example, Ben Jones lost his job last week and was fired on the spot.

Using this system in your student retention is critical. By having a system that allows you to monitor when they were last in class, you can keep an eye on the time elapsing between each session. Say a student decides to stop coming as they don't see progress, yet you can see they train once a month, you can suggest trying to dedicate themselves four times a month for a few months and then see how they feel. If they see positive change, which they will then encourage them to commit to the full ideal minimum of eight sessions a month. Once they start to feel the difference, you won't need to persuade them to come back anymore.

It's positive changes like these you can make to ensure each student is getting what they are supposed to from your school.

How do you track your students?

There are many student tracking applications provided by various software providers and billing companies. I like electronic tracking as it can feed into other reporting systems. In your school, you could choose between a modern or a traditional approach, but I think a combination of the two works well.

One impressive example is a Gracie Jiu-Jitsu school I visited in Miami. To track the attendance of their students, they had an iPad attached to the wall, and the students' merely touch the screen to say they were in class. I thought this was a brilliant system as it was low maintenance. You don't have to be a technology guru to manage it, and you don't require a person to be involved in tracking attendance physically.

I then saw all the students going over to the reception desk and picking out their attendance card from a box. At first, I was a little surprised, as I considered this quite an old school way of tracking attendance, and assumed it would be time-consuming. I then realised that there was much more to using the cards that met the eye.

What I saw next was a real light bulb moment for me. As the students were lined up ready to begin, they were looking at each other's cards discussing how much they'd been training, and what lessons had been covered. I heard phrases like "wow, you've been training a lot dude." and "I need to get down one more session a week as I missed lesson four twice this month."

The cards were a powerful retention tool in itself, and it didn't need external involvement. By comparing themselves to their peers, the students were inspired to do better to keep up with the achievements of those around them. If you create a culture within your school of commitment from the majority, the rest will follow suit.

By all means, use digital tracking apps for your overall data. Remember, a personal touch is vital. Your students are not numbers. Don't let them feel like one.

"Ah but Jon" I hear you ask, "three-weeks is quite a long time. By the time they are on the blacklist, it's probably too late." Fear not. There is a route to getting on the blacklist… enter the watchlist.

Have you ever been to the dentist for a check-up? I mean acted proactively, rather than waiting for a tooth to start aching. We've all been there. The dentist will prod and poke around your mouth and call out various words and codes to the dental nurse who sits tapping furiously on the keyboard. One of the phrases you are likely to hear is "let's put that tooth on a watch." Translation: there's no immediate action yet unless the patient (you) pays more attention to cleaning your teeth, and reducing your sugar intake then it might require more (painful and expensive) work in the future.

We apply the same technique to my school. After not having trained for 2-weeks, we put people on a watch. Students who are not attending initially go to the watchlist, and then may move to the blacklist. The watchlist means we are monitoring, finding out why they have not been training. The blacklist means we don't have any information, and therefore the students are at risk of leaving.

Both the watchlist and the blacklist are very dynamic. We run classes from Monday through to Saturday. Classing Saturday as the beginning of our training week, we update the lists on a Friday. The results dictate what actions we need to take the following week to get the students off the lists.

Once you've established both a watchlist and blacklist, the question then is how to stay in touch, and generate conversation with your students to motivate them to return to class.

Before I go into what does work, I'd like to approach the elephant in the room and discuss what doesn't. The "we missed you in class" call.

Calling your students, telling them you missed them in class and why didn't they train? This call often ends with a student quitting. I'm not surprised!

Putting someone on the spot out the blue can make them feel overwhelmed, uncomfortable, and embarrassed. Having to justify a lack of attendance throws them into a panicked state. One of which quitting becomes the quickest way to escape.

Instead, try calling them from a positive perspective. Give them a call and:

1. Ask their opinion on something.
2. Ask them to go through a quick member survey about the school.
3. Ask them to evaluate their goals and what is it they'd like to achieve?
4. Remind them of the free workshop coming up and that you're putting together a list of names of attendees.

By inspiring positivity, highlighting baby steps in the right direction, you can give them the nudge they need; without pressuring them. This will then minimise the names you see on your lists.

A proactive approach takes you to the next level and encourages students to stay focused training and that they need to make the class a priority in their hectic weekly schedule. There are four main things that I do:

Weekly email. I mentioned this earlier, I send a weekly email out to our active members with useful information about training, concepts of discipline, improvement or just recounting a story that has a valuable message. This email gets excellent feedback, and we can track who opens the email and watch their engagement with us.

School magazine/newsletter. We decided to send a full-colour 26-page magazine to all of our members eight times a year. We started off with a newsletter, then moved to the magazine. It arrives through their letterbox for them to read at home, at lunchtime or travelling to work. Our instructors and some of our members write articles, we list the upcoming events plus lots of training advice. This does take some focus and hard work but pushes you to the next level.

Online portal. Keeping members engaged when they are not on the mats is essential. Therefore we built our own members-only website that's packed full of video content, grading preparation advice, bodyweight training drills, and various other things that keep them engaged and focusing on their training.

Private Facebook Groups. Setting up private Facebook Groups is easy, posting regular content is not. We have a private group for each of our schools an endeavour to keep adding useful info, content, and follow-ups from training classes. This is the one which is simple to do, but consistency is tough because it relies on other people. Have a chat with your key members and ask for their support. If they post regularly, others will too. No one likes to go first. But then no one wants to feel left out either.

Of course, these methods take work. But you knew going into business you would need to make an effort to be successful. These seemingly insignificant actions are the steps that are going to transform you from good to great. There's a substantial difference between the two.

Every day, ask yourself: "What is the one thing I'm doing to do today to keep existing students and attract new ones?"

Create that ritual. Once the habits begin to form, you'll spend less time worrying, and will live a peaceful and more enjoyable existence. Focus on the basics, the stuff that keeps the engine running. Remember: discipline equals freedom.

CHAPTER CHECKPOINTS

How do you track attendance?

What is your process for dealing with no show students?

Do you balance keeping students with getting new students?

Chapter eighteen

Crisp grabbers.

"There is no need to be everything and do everything now. Take the time to focus and plan."

For many reasons, I've primarily focused my efforts on building successful adult krav maga schools. The most obvious being that as a self-defence method in close combat; you don't see many young children running around with weapons and knives in the western world. Or, at least you never used to. Thus, teaching krav maga to children wasn't as necessary.

When I first started, I knew of very few schools teaching children and they were predominantly based in Israel.

However, as times are changing, the risks concerning child safety are on the rise. Parents are looking for more practical alternatives to traditional martial arts disciplines to keep their child safe. Various social experiments have demonstrated how easy it can be for a predator to lure a child away from its safe environment and so parents need something that teaches their children to protect themselves against other children, but also against the risk posed by adults too.

A harsh reality to comprehend, but relevant to say the least.

A few years ago, the thought of ever teaching krav maga to children filled me with dread. You might say "But Jon, 70% of the martial arts market is training children." I get that, but it wasn't something I could bring myself to consider. That might have something to do with the fact that, at this moment in time I'm not a parent myself.

I'm used to teaching adults with clear goals. Police officers on a mission to improve their safety training. Military and governmental units who wish to enhance their defensive tactics skills. Blue chip companies who want conflict communication education for their front-line staff. I'm at the sharp end, so I had ZERO desire to enter into the realm of the crisp grabbers, (for my American friends, we mean potato chips) having them hanging off my arm and asking but why every two seconds. In truth, returning to Afghanistan appeared a more appealing idea!

However, one day someone convinced me teaching children would be far more rewarding than I expect it to be. And on the contrary, It wouldn't feel like I'm working in a soft play centre. Much to my surprise, I'm proud to say sometime later, Krav Maga Elite Kids was born; and we are not looking back. Although I had initially reluctantly agreed to teach children based on peer pressure from my team, one experience showed me the value of expanding our student base.

I was teaching a children's class one evening, and as usual, after finishing the class, I left the room to grab a bottle of water. In passing, I took a quick peek at the karate class on the other side of the hall. Now to be clear, I'm not disrespecting karate. In my opinion, when a defensive movement is more complicated than the attack you're facing, alarm bells start to ring if it's really a system of self-defence.

After watching the class, I saw most of the movements the children were learning seem pointless or unnecessary. Nevertheless, both the adults and kids did them anyway; without asking the instructor why.

I'm sure there is some answer that was relevant many years ago in Japan, but we're in a modern world. If you're marketing self-defence then simplicity and realism must be at the forefront of whatever is taught.

It was on that day I decided that the children we teach can ask the "why" question as much as they like. Understanding WHY they are doing a movement is so important if it's ever to be there for them if they need it, just as long as they don't grab my crisps when my attention is turned!

What I've learnt so far in my journey is that marketing for children's classes is profoundly different from adults. Your approach needs to change, your means and methods of communication will vary, and your retention strategies must take a different approach to adults. For one thing, you aren't marketing to an individual about their skills. You're targeting parents who are concerned about the welfare of their child and want to help them learn a valuable skill that will stay with them for life and support their development into positive human beings. Your message and approach will be entirely different than it will be for your adult school.

Designing a logo, renting a space, and getting a few children in the room to learn is not, in my opinion, the best way to set up a krav maga school for children. I'm not saying it's not a good idea. But from what I've seen, this seems to be the standard definition of running children's classes. I believe you can do better than that. Your children's school should be no less structured or professional than an adult school.

I really do believe that in the future, parents are going to be speaking to each other and asking "What krav maga class do your children go to?" in a similar fashion to asking which swimming club they're a part of. Both classes, of course, are valuable life skills that teach youngsters to deal with potentially dangerous situations.

While we aren't covering children's schools in this book, there is a trap many schools fall into that I feel obliged to raise awareness of. The profit vs programming method. Signing up children to your school is much easier than adults. If the parents see their little crisp grabber progressing, they will invest whatever time and money is required to make sure that continues. This must be respected at all times. Planning lessons, progress reporting, and awarding successes in a structured way is a must for training children; for the benefit of the child and their investor. Do not take what the parent has to go through to get the child to your class for granted. Create your training place in balance for the parents and the child, where the parent can feel happy leaving their child with you, or if they wish to stay, the training place is comfortable so they can take some time out to either watch the class, make calls or just take a 45 minute breaks from their hectic schedule.

I'd love to impart more wisdom on children schools right now, but you'll have to wait for the next book for that.

CHAPTER CHECKPOINTS

Do you run children's classes or do you run a children's school? (Hint: There is a difference and you should be aware of it)

How do you communicate with parents?

How do you reward success and report progress?

Chapter nineteen

My Hillary Step.

"Look up and keep going"

I've always been fascinated with climbing Mount Everest. It's not a goal per se. More so curiosity to understand what it takes to conquer it.

At its peak, the final ascent is a vertical rock face with a height of around 12 metres (39ft) located at approximately 8,790 metres (28,839ft) above sea level. For those not in the know, this is called the Hillary Step.

Recently in my career growing krav maga schools I've felt stuck on my Hillary Step. Looking up at my mountain, reluctant to climb to the top.

Until now, I'd actively decided not to open a full-time krav maga centre. We have an HQ office where my team work from, which has 70 square metres of matted space for instructor training and small courses, but it's an office with mats, it's not a showcase for my brand, it's a place for us to work from.

But if I'm going to take the step to the top, opening a full-time school and to build it in a way that can be replicated across locations of our choosing is my final ascent.

Many people who will be reading this will already have full-time training centres, and my hat is off to you for taking that step.

I've met many school owners who have invested in their own training space. Some have made huge successes, others have been buried in bills, empty mats, and napalmed the candle at both ends teaching class after class (after class).

Running satellite schools, classes that operate out of rented space per hour, has been enjoyable for me so far, only paying for space when I use it. That way, my overheads are low. I've not needed to worry about maintenance, parking, and other local taxes.

And to be completely honest, if I wasn't taking the crisps laden path of growing Krav Maga Elite Kids, I probably wouldn't be investing in a full-time centre. Why?

Because I didn't believe I needed to. With over 800 adult members in our brand across great UK-based locations, I perceived accumulating seemingly unnecessary overheads as nothing more than a way to haemorrhage cash-flow. Or is it?

The part about growing krav maga schools that I've loved most has been the initial struggle. Always moving forwards and upwards, having to work hard, finding out what works, building the systems.

I don't like endings. I hate when a project is finished, I love the process more than the end result. It might be stressful at times, but being uncomfortable is good. I might moan and groan I've got too much to do, but when I have nothing to do, I'm just as bad. Call me a maniac, but that's what drives me.

One of my most significant failings in business is not celebrating success enough. Do not follow my lead on this. When you achieve a goal and succeed, no matter how small, take the time to celebrate the little wins. Yes, the big lofty ones are an incredible achievement, but more often than not, it's the smaller successes that got you there. It's not about the destination; it's the journey that counts.

We recently gave notice on our HQ office and have just signed the lease on a new place where we will formally launch our children's programme.

It has taken me a long time to make this decision. I did not want to follow all of the school owners I've met with lots of mat space. Those keeping the lights on all day but not enough students to pay for it.

I wanted to be sure of our systems. From financial to sales. Marketing and customer service. Everything I feel is necessary that leaves us free to focus on teaching exceptional krav maga. I wanted to focus on following my own learnings laid out in this book to take the next step up.

Opening your own training space is a big step, and is the ultimate dream of many school owners. Luckily I have some very supportive people around me who've advised on lease agreements, location, space, layout, and much more. There are people around you who know more about building out premises; I'll remind you that you're not the plumber, you might end up handing out the tools to get your hands a little dirty, but make sure you speak to the right people if that's the route you're going.

I think deep down I know that if I don't take this route, I'll be forever standing on my Hillary Step endlessly looking up.

It's often said to look forward and not back, but I prefer to look up. I guess that's the advice when climbing Everest. When I look up the possibilities are endless. Setting up a full-time centre for both children and adults. One that's vibrant, packed full of members, and locally known as the go-to place for krav maga training has to be the summit.

It's going to cost some money and time. There will be pressures, stresses and some heated words along the way. But with the right team, the right attitude, asking smart questions to the right people and with a clear focus; it will happen.

My point of sharing my ramblings with you is to encourage you to analyse where you are now. Where are you compared to where to be?

Is what you're doing now, how you're living day-to-day representative of what you wanted to set-up?

If you're working full-time and also running a school part-time, do you dream of being full-time? And if so what needs to change for you to achieve that?

Do you have a full-time centre but it's not running at full capacity and if so, what parts of this book do you need to focus on?

Is it the financial numbers?

Is it your website and marketing?

Is it your sales process and how you communicate?

Do you need a bigger or better team?

Or do you need to re-evaluate your why?

Is something in your process stuck? Which part is it? Analyse it, be clear, and make changes. It might be scary, but it's also more straightforward than you might think.

If you can hand on heart say after reading this book that you are exactly where you want to be and you're achieving all you set out to, I admire you, and I'd love to invite you for a coffee.

For the most part, and pardon me for being presumptuous, but I'll take a punt at the fact you aren't there yet.

You've got another goal, another plan. To grow to expand, to go bigger and share what you know with even more people. This is called entrepreneurship. It's addictive. But there are far worst things to be addicted to.

Keep doing what you're doing, learning, expanding, and helping the world become better.

CHAPTER CHECKPOINTS

Where are you in relation to where you want to be?

Are you focussed on the future or dwelling in the past?

What is the most significant change you could make to take you another step up?

Epilogue

"Make the most of your remaining months.
There are no second chances."

If you had picked up this book and expected to find a long list of things to do to get you a few new members or some fancy new way to run Facebook ads, then I'm sorry to have disappointed you.

Don't fall into the trap of over analysing everyone else and searching for the perfect solution and taking advice from unsuccessful people. Let me save you the hassle. I did that.

As we say in krav maga training, Stop. Think and scan the area to make sure you've got your plan laid out. You already know enough to move forward, it just needs to be organised into something that you can follow.

Before trying to pile more on your plate and looking for the next big thing to improve your school. Take a moment. Look at what you have and make a conscious effort to fix what you have. Only then can you move forward.

The plan that's right is the one that suits you. The one that gets you the results you desire. That always comes back to your big why. You should be asking yourself: "What is most important to me?" "How do I define my success?"

I've mentioned this a couple of times in this book, but this being the last chapter, I want to draw your attention to time management as it's the most critical thing you can nurture. I'm no expert, but I act conscientiously.

Think about it. If you live to the age of 90, you'll have lived for 1,080 months. Doesn't sound very long, does it? Which means as I write this at the age of 40, I've got around 600 months left before I must kick in those pearly gates with a jumping front kick.

The mistake is that many people often prioritise what appears to be urgent, over what is essential. Then end up having no time. Urgency occurs typically on somebody else's time. Having somebody else govern your time is, in my view, a miserable existence.

In many cases, their slipping deadline is not your concern. I don't leave things to the last minute, and I don't expect others to pick up the load if I do because it's now become urgent.

Of course, there are some things which are urgent and essential, but if you're categorising something as such, be entirely sure it's critical. If not, downgrade it.

Your focus must be on things that are important to your business and personal life. What are the five most important things you can do today? The five things that will move you towards your goals. List them and then go and achieve them. Then move on to the other not so important things, that make your daily life that little bit easier.

Schedule the core daily chores in your life; exercise, cooking, cleaning, the school run etc. Believe me, scheduling is a powerful tool, and it helps you by eliminating the number of decisions you have to make. Better still, get to a position where you can 'outsource' the tasks that fill your time so you can focus on what's most important. If a cleaner for your house costs you £10 per hour, and you can make £100 per hour, it's a no-brainer. Do you need to do it? Can somebody else do it better than you or, that will cost you less than you can make? That's smart thinking.

When you schedule your core activity, you'll stick to it. For example, I work out with a personal trainer, this is a pre-scheduled appointment which I'm paying for, so you'd better believe that I am going to move heaven and earth to be there. The upside of this technique is that I don't have to think about fitting it in or deciding whether I can afford the time to go. It's set. I turn up and work out. Simple.

Many of your beliefs around how you should live your life will come from your upbringing and the opinions of your parents. These are scripted subconscious patterns. You can either choose to follow them or break them, but you need to be aware of them.

If you were raised being told you need "to do a hard days work and pay your bills", in principle, the advice is sound, but taken to the extreme, it can be debilitating and limiting.

I believe we were put on this planet to expand, build, grow, and help others.

Your krav maga school is a place where you can do that. It's your opportunity to create a place of positivity. Where people can learn a life skill to deal with the few people who don't buy into the help others attitude. At the same time helping them get fitter, stronger, instil them with confidence, and create a positive environment filled with like-minded people and admirable values.

That's a severe responsibility you've got there, take it seriously.

Work with the right people, take the time to find the best ones, and remove the rotten apples quickly.

Stay true to your values and nurture your time like the way you would your vulnerable newborn baby. Protect it at all costs.

I hope this book was of use. It's merely my thoughts, learnings, and experiences. It doesn't mean it's the path you absolutely must follow but more a guide in the right direction.

I've added my checklist to krav maga success. Scan the list. What is most relevant to you right now?

Life is about finding your own path, being clear on the destination, and making sure you spend time with amazing people and help as many of them as you can. Life is the ultimate adventure, seize the most out of it.

If we've met before, thank you for the conversation and shared insight. If we haven't met yet, I look forward to it.

Here's to your krav maga success.

MY CHECKLIST FOR KRAV MAGA SUCCESS:

- Control your diary: guard your time.
- Plan your priorities, what is most important?
- Monitor your cash, know your numbers.
- Know your values and make decisions by them.
- Spend time with the right type of people. Cut away from those who do not support you.
- Slow down when speaking to others, allow more time for listening and processing.
- Don't just buy books, study them.
- Control your personal spending, invest in the long term.
- Fire yourself. Delegate to others better than you.
- A meeting must have a goal. Share that with others.
- Think long-term, be patient.
- Be aware of fear. Certain fears have patterns.
- Not everyone thinks like you.
- Review, review, review. What's working and what is not?
- Pay for the right advice and guidance and be sure to implement the learning.
- Be consistent, create useful habits.
- Create a balance between training, coaching, and business.
- There is no growth in comfort; embrace change.
- Look up, that's your next step.

Finally, and most importantly. Enjoy it. This is your journey.

For more support and guidance join the conversation at our Facebook group *www.facebook.com/groups/kravmagasuccess*

About the Author

Jon Bullock is an expert level instructor with Krav Maga Global. He is a member of their international training team and the director of training for the United Kingdom.

He is responsible for the growth of krav maga in the UK and facilitates instructor certification programmes, further development opportunities, and school owner support systems.

Jon is also the founder of Krav Maga Elite – Self Defence & Fitness. A UK-based provider of krav maga training, operating weekly classes across the UK to both adults and children. At the time of writing, Krav Maga Elite has over 800 active members.

Jon has also provided bespoke defensive tactics and conflict de-escalation training programmes, to various police forces, government departments, Military units, and global companies worldwide.

Jon lives in Chelmsford, Essex with his partner Helen and can be contacted via email on success@kravmagaelite.co.uk.